ALL AMERICAN STORIES

C. G. DRAPER

Longman

All American Stories C

Pearson Education, 10 Bank Street, White Plains, NY 10606

Vice president, primary and secondary editorial: Ed Lamprich
Senior development editor: Lauren Weidenman
Vice president, director of design and production: Rhea Banker
Executive managing editor: Linda Moser
Production editor: Lynn Contrucci
Senior art director: Elizabeth Carlson
Vice president, marketing: Kate McLoughlin
Senior manufacturing buyer: Edith Pullman
Cover design: Lissi Sigillo
Cover art: Edward Hopper, Lighthouse at Two Lights, 1929. Oil on canvas. Photo from The
    Granger Collection, New York.
Text design: Elizabeth Carlson
Text composition: Rainbow Graphics
Text fonts: Franklin Gothic Book and Minion
Text credit: "A Day's Wait" reprinted with permission of Scribner, an imprint of Simon &
    Schuster Adult Publishing Group, from *The Short Stories of Ernest Hemingway*. Copyright
    1933 by Charles Scribner's Sons. Copyright renewed © 1961 by Mary Hemingway.
Illustrations: John Edens: "Rip Van Winkle"; Tom LaPadula: "April Showers"; Rob Lawson: "A
    White Heron"; Isidre Mones: "The Cask of Amontillado"; Kevin McCain: "A Day's Wait";
    Tim Otis: "A Mystery of Heroism"; Gonzalez Vicente: "Hope Deferred"

Library of Congress Cataloging-in-Publication Data

All American stories / [edited] by C. G. Draper.
        p. cm.
    Includes index.
    ISBN 0-13-192990-9
    1. English language—Textbooks for foreign speakers. 2. Short stories,
American—Adaptations. 3. Readers (Secondary) I. Draper, C. G.
PE1128.A365 2006
428.6'4—dc22

                                                        2004026234

LONGMAN ON THE **WEB**

Longman.com offers online resources for
teachers and students. Access our Companion
Websites, our online catalog, and our local
offices around the world.

Visit us at **longman.com.**

Printed in the United States of America
3 4 5 6 7 8 9 10—ML—10 09 08 07 06

Contents

To the Student

The stories in this book were written many years ago by seven of America's most famous writers. Some words and sentences in most of the stories have been changed. These changes make the stories easier to understand for students learning English as a second language. The stories begin at the intermediate level of English language proficiency and end at the advanced level.

The introductory unit—"What Is a Short Story?"—is different from Units 1 to 6. It will help you understand how to read a short story. It explains the words **characters, plot, setting,** and **theme.** It also points out details about these features as it takes you through a story called "A White Heron" by Sarah Orne Jewett.

In Units 1 to 6, you will find:

- A paragraph about the life of the person who wrote the story.

- A section called "Before You Read." This section introduces you to the story. It gives you important background information. And it tells you the meaning of some words that are important in the story.

- The story itself and pictures that help you understand the story.

- A section called "After You Read." This section contains reading comprehension questions, discussion questions, and an extension activity. It also includes exercises in vocabulary and word study, and gives you practice in writing. In addition, this section gives you activities to help you understand the elements of literature.

Reading this book will help you improve many English language skills: reading, speaking, listening, and writing. You will also learn many things about American history and about the daily life of the country's people many years ago.

Good luck, and good reading!

What Is a Short Story?

Short stories can be different lengths. But most short stories have the following things in common: **characters, plot, setting,** and **theme.** These are called the elements of a short story.

The people in a story are its **characters.** A good writer creates characters that seem like real people. You care about them and read to find out what happens to them.

The story's **plot** is what happens to the characters. The plot can focus on one event or include many events.

The **setting** is where and when the story happens. Some stories can happen anywhere, at any time. Other stories can happen only in a specific place and time.

The **theme** is a general idea about life that the author communicates by telling the story. Some stories do not have a theme.

The model story is "A White Heron" by Sarah Orne Jewett. Following are descriptions of its elements.

Characters
Sylvia, a young man, Sylvia's grandmother

Plot
Sylvia meets a stranger who is hunting birds. He asks to stay at her family's home for the night. Sylvia's grandmother lets him stay, but Sylvia is afraid. The man is hunting a white heron. Sylvia knows how to find this bird. But will she tell the stranger where the white heron lives?

Setting
Time: June
Place: the woods in Maine

Theme
It's not easy to choose between two things you love.

Character

Authors help you get to know their characters in different ways. They can describe what the characters look like. They can tell you what the characters do and say. Authors can also tell you what the characters are thinking and feeling.

Characters in a short story often learn something as a result of what happens in the story. The way a character develops, or changes, during the story can usually tell you something about the story's meaning.

In "A White Heron," the main character is Sylvia. At the beginning of the story, Sylvia is afraid of strangers. As you read the story, you will see how Sylvia's feelings change.

Plot

The plot is the story's action, or what happens. It is a series of events that lead from one to the other. The author usually tells the story in the order in which the events happened. This is called **chronological order,** or time order.

At the center of most plots is a **conflict,** or a problem. The conflict can be between two characters. Or it can be between a character and nature, as in a story about someone who gets sick. Sometimes the conflict is inside a character, such as when the character has to make a difficult choice.

In "A White Heron," Sylvia's feelings are in conflict. Sylvia's conflict is resolved at the end of the story in a surprising way.

Setting

The place and the time of a story is its setting. Place might be a city or a person's home. Time might be a period in history or the time of year.

Sometimes an author tells you the setting of a story right away. Often an author tells you about the setting little by little as the story unfolds.

Sometimes setting is important to a story, but this is not always true. If the author calls attention to the setting often, then it is probably important.

"A White Heron" is set in Maine, in June. Certain details tell you that the story takes place long ago. For example, when the young man offers Sylvia $10, she can't believe anyone could have so much money. Today, most people wouldn't think that $10 is a lot of money.

Theme

The theme is the central idea or message that the story conveys. The theme usually makes you think about life in general.

In some stories, the author includes a sentence that tells you the theme. The sentence might be something the narrator or another character says. In most stories, however, the author wants you to figure out the theme. In order to do this, you usually need to think about the story for a while. Try to state the theme in your own words. This can help you understand the story better and enjoy it more.

The theme of "A White Heron" is that choosing between two things you love is not easy.

A White Heron

Adapted from the story by Sarah Orne Jewett

I

Setting: The story is set in the woods. The main character, Sylvia, feels a part of the woods. She comes alive in "this beautiful place."

The woods were already filled with shadows one June evening just before eight o'clock. Sylvia was driving her cow home. They turned deep into the dark woods. Their feet knew the way. The birds in the trees above her head seemed to sing "good night" to each other quietly. The air was soft and sweet. Sylvia felt a part of the gray shadows and the moving leaves. To Sylvia, it seemed as if she hadn't really been alive before she came to live with her grandmother in this beautiful place.

Plot: The second paragraph sets the plot in motion. Sylvia meets a young man, a stranger.

Suddenly she heard a call. Not a bird's call, which would have had a friendly sound. It was a young man's call, sudden and loud. Sylvia left the cow alone and hid behind some leaves. But the young man saw her.

"Halloa, little girl. How far is it to the road?"

Sylvia was afraid. She answered in a soft voice, "A good ways . . ." She did not dare to look directly at the tall young man. But she came out from behind the leaves and followed the cow. The young man walked alongside them.

Character: Sylvia is not afraid to walk alone in the woods. Yet she is afraid of this young man. She is more at ease with the shadows and the trees than she is with people.

"I'm hunting for some birds," the young man said kindly. He carried a gun over his shoulder. "I am lost and need a friend very much. Don't be afraid. Speak up, and tell me what your name is. Do you think I can spend the night at your house and go out hunting in the morning?"

Character: The author compares Sylvia with a "broken flower." This tells you that Sylvia is fragile, or easily broken.

Sylvia was more afraid than ever. Her grandmother would probably be angry if this stranger followed her home. But she said her name and dropped her head like a broken flower.

Her grandmother was waiting at the door. The cow gave a "moo" as the three arrived.

"Yes, you should speak for yourself, you old cow," said her grandmother. "Where was she hiding so long, Sylvy?"

Sylvia didn't speak. She thought her grandmother should be afraid of the stranger.

But the young man stood his gun beside the door. He dropped a heavy gun-bag beside it. He said good evening and told the old woman his story.

"Dear me, yes," she answered. "You might do better if you went out to the road a mile away. But you're welcome to what we've got. I'll milk the cow right away. Now, you make yourself at home. Sylvy, step around, and set a plate for the gentleman!"

Sylvia stepped. She was glad to have something to do, and she was hungry.

The young man was surprised to find such a comfortable, clean house in the deep woods of Maine. He thought this was the best supper he had eaten in a month. After supper the new-made friends sat in the shadowed doorway to watch the moon come up. The young man listened happily to the grandmother's stories. The old woman talked most about her children. About her daughter, Sylvia's mother, who had a hard life with so many children. About her son, Dan, who left home for California many years ago.

"Sylvy is like Dan," she said happily. "She knows every foot of the woods. She plays with the woods animals and feeds the birds. Yes, she'd give her own meals to them, if I didn't watch her!"

"So Sylvy knows all about birds, does she?" asked the young man. "I am trying to catch one of every kind. I have been doing it ever since I was a boy."

"Do you keep them alive?" asked the old woman.

"No. I stuff them in order to save them," he answered. "I have almost a hundred of them. And I caught every one myself."

Sylvia was watching a toad jump in the moonlight.

"I followed a bird here that I want to catch. A white heron. You

Plot: Sylvia's fear makes you wonder about the stranger. What does he want? Can he be trusted?

Character: Sylvia's grandmother is not afraid of the young man at all. She is very friendly to him. Sylvia seems even shyer in comparison.

Character: Sylvia spends her time playing with the animals in the woods. She doesn't seem to have any other friends.

Plot: Now you know why the young man is hunting the bird. He wants to kill it and stuff it.

would know a heron if you saw it, Sylvy," he said, hopefully. "A strange, tall white bird with long, thin legs. Its nest would be in the top of a high tree, like a hawk's nest."

Sylvia's heart stopped. She knew that strange white bird.

"I want that bird more than anything," the young man went on. "I would give ten dollars to know where its nest is."

Sylvia couldn't believe there was so much money in the world. But she watched the toad and said nothing.

The next day Sylvia went with the young man into the woods. He was kind and friendly, and told her many things about the birds. He spoke in a soft voice so as not to scare the birds away. From time to time they stopped to listen to a bird's song. And the young man gave Sylvia his own knife to use in the woods. She thought of it as a great treasure.

She wasn't afraid of him anymore. Perhaps in her heart a dream of love was born. But she couldn't understand why he killed and stuffed the birds he liked so much.

II

At the edge of the woods a great pine tree stood. Sylvia knew it well. That night she thought of the tree. If she climbed it early in the morning, she could see the whole world. Couldn't she watch the heron fly, and find its hidden nest? What an adventure it would be! And how happy her friend would be! The young man and the old woman slept well that night, but Sylvia thought of her adventure. She forgot to think of sleep. At last, when the night birds stopped singing, she quietly left the house.

There was the tall pine tree, still asleep in the moonlight. First she climbed a smaller tree next to it. Then she made the dangerous step across to the old pine. The birds in the woods below her were waking up. She must climb faster if she wanted to see the heron as it left its nest. The tree seemed to grow taller as she went up. The pine tree must have been surprised to feel this small person climbing up.

Plot: Sylvia's idea that ten dollars is such a large sum of money tells you that she and her grandmother are poor. It also tells you that the story takes place long ago, when ten dollars was worth a lot more than it is today.

Character/Plot: Sylvia's feelings have changed since the beginning of the story. She is starting to love the stranger. But Sylvia has a conflict: She loves the young man, but she also loves the birds.

Setting: The author describes the pine tree as though it is a person. This is the way Sylvia thinks of it. The tree is her friend. Giving a thing, such as a tree, human traits is called **personification.**

It must have loved this new animal in its arms. Perhaps it moved its branches a little, to help her climb. Sylvia's face shone like a star when she reached the top. She was tired, but very happy. She could see ships out to sea. Woods and farms lay for miles and miles around her. The birds sang louder and louder. At last the sun came up. Where was the heron's nest? Look, look, Sylvia! A white spot rises up from the green trees below. The spot grows larger. The heron flies close. A wild, light bird, wide wings, and a long thin neck. He stops in the tree beyond Sylvia. Wait, wait, Sylvia! Do not move a foot or a finger, to frighten it away!

A moment later, Sylvia sighs. A large company of noisy birds comes to the tree, and the heron goes away. It flies down to its home in the green world below. Sylvia knows its secret now. She climbs back down. Her fingers hurt, and her feet slip. She wonders what the young man will say to her. What will he think when she tells him how to find the heron's nest?

"Sylvy, Sylvy!" her grandmother called, but nobody answered.

The young man woke up and dressed. He wanted to begin hunting again. He was sure Sylvia knew something about the white heron. Here she comes now. Her small face is white, her old dress is torn and dirty. The grandmother and the young man wait at the door to question her. The time has come to tell about the heron's nest.

But Sylvia does not speak. The young man looks into her eyes. He will make them rich. She wants to make him happy. He waits to hear the story she can tell.

No, she must keep silent! What is it that keeps her quiet? This is the first time the world has put out a hand to her. Does she have to push it away because of a bird? She hears the wind blowing in the pine tree. She remembers how the white heron flew through the golden air. She remembers how they watched the sea and the morning together. Sylvia cannot speak. She cannot tell the heron's secret and give its life away.

Poor Sylvia! She was sad when the young man went away. She

Plot: The author lets you think that Sylvia will tell the young man about the heron. But she does not speak. She chooses not to harm the heron.

Plot: The author shows you how Sylvia argues with herself. She is trying to make the right choice.

could have helped him. She would have followed him like a dog. She would have loved him as a dog loves! Many nights afterwards Sylvia remembered his "Halloa" as she came home with the cow. She forgot the sadness she felt whenever she heard the sharp sound of his gun. She forgot seeing the birds, wet with blood, and wanting to cry. Were the birds better friends than the hunter? Who can tell?

Oh, Woods! Oh, Summertime! Remember what riches were lost to her. Bring her your riches instead, your beauties and your gifts. Tell all your secrets to this lonely country child! ⌒

1

The Cask of Amontillado

Adapted from the story by Edgar Allan Poe

About the Author

Edgar Allan Poe was born in 1809 in Boston, Massachusetts. His parents died when he was a child. Poe was raised by John and Frances Allan, in Richmond, Virginia. He quarreled with the Allans when he was a young man and left home. Poe worked as an editor for several literary magazines but lost his job frequently. His own writing—poetry and short stories—became popular, but he remained poor in spite of his literary success. He died in 1849. Poe is generally considered the first writer of mystery or detective stories. "The Murders of the Rue Morgue" and "The Gold Bug" are among these. He is equally famous for the horror stories—such as "The Tell-Tale Heart" and "The Cask of Amontillado"—in which he explores the dark side of the human mind and heart.

Before You Read

About "The Cask of Amontillado"

Characters
Montressor, the narrator; Fortunato

Plot
Montressor is angry because Fortunato has insulted him. One evening during Carnival, Montressor decides to get his revenge. Curiously, the reader never learns what Fortunato had done to insult Montressor. Poe leaves that part of the plot for the reader to think about.

Setting
Time: early 1800s, during Carnival season
Place: city streets, underground vaults in Montressor's house

Theme
The desire for revenge is a powerful human feeling.

Build Background

Amontillado and Carnival

Amontillado (ah-mon-tee-YAH-doe) is a type of wine. A cask is a large barrel that, usually, contains wine. The most famous Amontillado comes from Spain. Yet we cannot be sure that this story is set in Spain. Certainly it is set in a country that, like Spain or Italy, has a Carnival season. At Carnival time, there is feasting and merrymaking. Carnival comes right before Lent, a period of strict religious observance.

Many cultures have a period of feasting and merrymaking. What kinds of similar celebrations do you know of in a country outside the United States?

Key Words

Read these sentences. Try to understand each word in boldfaced type by looking at the other words in the sentence. Use a dictionary to check your ideas. Write each word and its meaning in your notebook.

damp
mold
noble
palazzo
torch

1. Montressor's vaults are **damp**—the walls and the ground are slightly wet.

2. The walls of Montressor's vaults are covered with **mold,** a fungus that grows on damp surfaces.

3. A person who is **noble** has a high moral character or a high social standing.

4. Montressor lives in a **palazzo.** He has many servants who take care of his large house.

5. Montressor lights a **torch.** Its fire helps him see in the dark.

Reading Strategy

Make Inferences

When you **make inferences,** or **infer,** you make reasonable guesses based on information in the story and your own knowledge. For example, read this passage from the story:

> Putting on a mask of black silk in order to mix with the Carnival crowd, I allow him to hurry me to my palazzo.

From the information in this sentence, you can infer that people wear masks during Carnival. You can also infer that the streets are crowded with people.

Poe does not explain everything in "The Cask of Amontillado." Some parts of the story will be hard to understand unless you make inferences as you read.

The Cask of Amontillado

Adapted from the story by Edgar Allan Poe

I

I had born the thousand injuries of Fortunato[1] as well as I could, but when he dared to insult me, I knew I must have revenge.

However, you, my friend, will understand that I never spoke a threat. I, Montressor,[2] would have revenge eventually; there was no doubt about that. But I wanted no risk. I wanted to punish, but to punish in safety, and with confidence. The insult would be paid back, yes. But also the insulter must know the punisher. And Montressor, the punisher, must go free.

I continued, therefore, to smile in Fortunato's face, as always. He could not know that my smile *now* was at the thought of his destruction.

He had a weakness, this Fortunato. He was proud of his knowledge of wines. In fact, he did know the old Italian wines very well—as I did. And this was excellent for my purposes.

It was about dusk, one evening during Carnival, when I found him walking along the crowded street. He greeted me with unusual warmth, for he had been drinking much. The man wore Carnival clothes: a brightly colored shirt, tight pants, and a hat with little bells on it. I was so pleased to see him that I almost forgot to let go of his hand.

"My dear Fortunato," I said, "how well you look! But what do you think? I have received a cask of the real Amontillado wine. At least they *say* it's the real thing. But I have my doubts."

"What, Montressor?" said he. "Amontillado? A whole cask? Impossible! And in the middle of Carnival!"

[1] *Fortunato* (for-choo-NAH-toe)
[2] *Montressor* (mon-tress-SORE)

"I have my doubts," I repeated. "And do you know, I was foolish enough to pay the full Amontillado price. I had to do it without asking you. I couldn't find you, and I didn't want to lose a bargain."

"Amontillado!"

"I have my doubts."

"Amontillado!"

"And I must bury them."

"Amontillado!"

"Since you are busy, I am going to find Luchresi.[3] If anyone has the ability to judge, it is he. He will tell me—"

"Luchresi cannot tell the difference between Amontillado and ordinary wine."

"And yet some fools say that his taste is equal to yours."

"Come, let us go."

"Where?"

"To your vaults."

"My friend, no. I refuse to give you trouble in this way. I see that you are on your way to a party. Luchresi—"

"I am going nowhere. Come."

"My friend, no. It is not only the party. I see you have a bad cold. My vaults are terribly damp. You will suffer."

"Let us go anyway. My cold is nothing. And Luchresi? I tell you, the man cannot tell Amontillado from milk!"

Speaking in this way, Fortunato took my arm. Putting on a mask of black silk in order to mix with the Carnival crowd, I allowed him to hurry me to my palazzo.[4]

There were no servants at home; they were all enjoying the Carnival. I had told them that I would not return to the palazzo until the morning. To them, this announcement was like an invitation to go on vacation.

I took two torches from their holders. Giving one to Fortunato, I led him through many rooms. We came to the door that led into the vaults. We walked through it and down a long and winding staircase. I requested him continuously to be careful. At last we came to the

---

[3] *Luchresi* (loo-CRAY-zee)
[4] *palazzo* (pah-LAHT-so)

bottom and stood on the damp ground of the burial vaults of my family, the Montressors.

II

The footsteps of my friend were unsteady, and the bells on his hat lightly rang as he walked.

"The cask?" said he.

"It is a little further," I said. "But look at the white mold on the walls down here."

He turned toward me unsteadily. I saw in his eyes how much he had been drinking.

"What did you say?" he asked.

"Mold," I repeated, "the mold on the walls. How long have you had that bad cough?"

"Ugh! ugh! ugh!—ugh! ugh! ugh!—ugh! ugh! ugh! ugh! ugh!—ugh! ugh! ugh!"

My poor friend could not reply for many minutes.

"It is nothing," he said at last.

"Come," I said with decision, "we will go back. Your health is precious. You are rich, admired, loved. You are happy, as I once was. You are a man who will be missed. For me, it is no matter. We will go back; you will be ill, and I cannot be responsible. Besides, there is Luchresi—"

"Enough!" he said. "The cough is a mere nothing; it will not kill me. I shall not die of a cough."

"True, true," I replied. "And indeed I did not mean to frighten you. But you must use proper caution. A drink of this fine Medoc wine will protect us from the dampness."

Here, I broke off the neck of a bottle which I took from a long row that lay on the mold.

"Drink," I said, giving him the wine.

He raised it to his lips with a smile that I did not like.

He said, "I drink to the members of your fine family who are buried in these vaults."

"And I drink to your long life," I quietly replied. Again he took my arm and we continued. The wine shone in his eyes. My own face was warm with the Medoc. We were deeper into the vaults now, and began to pass piles of human bones. I took Fortunato by an arm above the elbow.

"Look! The mold," I said. "See, it increases. It hangs from the roof of the vault. We must be below the river. That is why the dampness is so bad. Come, we will go back before it is too late. Your cough—"

"It is nothing," he said; "let us continue. But first another drink of the Medoc." He finished the wine in one swallow. Then he threw the bottle into the air with a strange motion that I did not understand. He repeated the motion again. His eyes questioned me, but I could only look at him in surprise.

"You do not understand the sign?" he said.

"No," I replied.

"Then you are not a Mason."

"A mason?" I said. "Isn't a mason someone who builds walls?"

"Ha! I mean a member of our secret society. We are called Masons. Have you never heard of us and our secret meetings?"

"Ah, yes, a mason," I said. "I am indeed a mason."

"You? Impossible! A Mason?"

"A real mason," I replied.

"Prove it," said he. "Give me the secret sign!"

"It is this," I answered. From a large pocket inside my coat I took a small tool. It was a trowel, used by masons to put plaster between the bricks in a wall.

"Ha! ha! You joke," he said. "Excellent! Now come. Let us continue to the Amontillado."

"Indeed," I said, and offered him my arm again. He leaned on it heavily. We passed through more rooms of bottles, casks, and bones. We went down one more staircase and arrived at last in the deepest room of the vaults. Here the human bones were piled as high as the ceiling. It was very dark, and our torches glowed rather weakly. At the far end of the large room there was still another, smaller room. It lay beyond an opening of one meter in width.

"Continue," I said. "The Amontillado is in there. I wonder whether Luchresi—"

"He is a fool," my friend said as he stepped unsteadily forward into the last small room. I followed quickly after him. His progress was stopped by the bare wall ahead of him, which he looked at stupidly in confusion. In a moment I had chained him to the rock. On its surface were two iron rings, about two feet apart. A short chain hung from one of these rings, and a lock from the other. Throwing the chain quickly twice around his waist, I took only a few seconds to attach it to the lock. He was too astonished to struggle against me. Taking the key of the lock with me, I stepped back from the small room.

"If you place your hand on the wall," I said, "you will feel the mold. Indeed it is *very* damp. Once more I *beg* you to return with me. No? Then I must leave you. But first I should try to make you as comfortable as possible."

"The Amontillado!" cried my friend. He was not yet recovered from his astonishment.

"True," I replied; "the Amontillado."

As I said these words, I walked to the nearest small pile of bones. I began moving aside those on the top. Soon I uncovered some plaster and building stone. With these materials and with the help of my trowel, I began energetically to wall up the entrance to the small room.

I had laid only the first row of stones when I discovered that the effects of Fortunato's drinking had disappeared. The first sign of this was a low continual groan from the small room. It was not simply the groan of a man who has been drinking too much. Then there was a long and insistent silence. I laid the second row, and the third, and the fourth. And then I heard a furious shaking of the chains. I sat down and listened to it with satisfaction until it stopped. Then I finished the fifth, the sixth, and the seventh row. The wall was now at the height of my chest. I again paused, and holding my torch above the wall, I threw the light on the figure inside.

Loud, terrible screams burst from the throat of that chained form. They seemed to push me violently backward. For a brief moment I hesitated. But when I placed my hand on the strong walls of the vault, I again felt satisfied. I approached the wall a second time. I replied to the screams with screams of my own. I echoed and reechoed the man, passing him in loudness and strength. I did this, and the screaming stopped.

My work was almost finished. I had completed the eighth, the ninth, and the tenth row. I had finished the eleventh, except for the final stone. I struggled with its weight; I had it almost into position. But now a low laugh came from the small room—a laugh that horrified me. It was followed by a sad voice, which I had difficulty recognizing as the voice of the noble Fortunato. The voice said—

"Ha! ha! ha!-he! he! he!—a very good joke indeed—an excellent joke! We will have much laughter about it at the palazzo—he! he! he!—over our wine!—he! he! he!"

"The Amontillado," I said.

"He! he! he!—he! he! he!—yes, the Amontillado. But it is getting late. Won't they be waiting for us at the palazzo, the Lady Fortunato and the rest? Let us be gone."

"Yes," I said, "let us be gone."

"Why? Why? For the love of God, Montressor! You're mad!"

"Yes," I said, "for the love of God!"

But there was no reply to these words. I waited. I called—

"Fortunato!"

No answer. I called again—

"Fortunato!"

No answer still. I placed a torch through the last hole and let it fall inside. Only a small ringing of bells came in return. My heart grew sick; it was the dampness of the vault. I hurried now in finishing. I forced the last stone into its position; I plastered it. I put the pile of old bones in front of the new wall. And for half a century, no man has disturbed them.

In pace requiescat![5] 〰

---

[5]*In pace requiescat!*: Latin for "May he rest in peace!"

After You Read

Understand the Story

Answer these questions in your notebook. Write complete sentences.

1. Who is the narrator of this story?
2. What holiday was it when Montressor and Fortunato met on the street?

   Fortunate

3. What did Montressor tell Fortunato he had received?
4. Where did the two men go, and why?

   a gieft

5. What "sign" did Fortunato give Montressor?

   palazzo

6. What did Montressor do to Fortunato when the two men reached the last room underground? Why did he do it?

   sad

   he killed him, so he can get the final level

Elements of Literature

Characterization

Read this quote from Fortunato. Then answer the questions.

> "Luchresi cannot tell the difference between Amontillado and ordinary wine. . . . I tell you, the man cannot tell Amontillado from milk!"

How do Fortunato's words show his pride? In what way does Fortunato's pride contribute to his death?

Discussion

Discuss in pairs or small groups.

1. What was your reaction to "The Cask of Amontillado"? Were you satisfied—or horrified—that Montressor got his revenge on Fortunato? Did the story amuse you? Scare you? Entertain you?

2. In the end, what do you think Montressor feels about the revenge he takes on Fortunato? Explain your answer.

Vocabulary

Choose the correct word. Write the completed sentences in your notebook.

1. I had told the servants that I would not return to my __B__ until the morning.
   a. torch   **b.** palazzo   **c.** Carnival

2. "I see you have a bad cold. My vaults are terribly __C__. You will suffer."
   a. damp   **b.** noble   **c.** mold

3. "Look at the white __A__ on the walls down here . . . it hangs from the roof of the vault."
   a. noble   **b.** mold   **c.** damp

4. It was very dark, and our __C__ glowed rather weakly.
   a. casks   **b.** palazzos   **c.** torches

5. I had difficulty recognizing the voice of the __B__ Fortunato.
   a. noble   **b.** torch   **c.** mold

Word Study

Adverbs are words that tell you how something happens. Adverbs are often made by adding *-ly* to the **adjective** form of a word.

Write the sentences below in your notebook. Complete each sentence with the correct form of the word. Use the chart to help you. The first one has been done for you.

Adjective	Adverb
bright	brightly
light	lightly
terrible	terribly
unsteady	unsteadily
quick	quickly
secret	secretly

1. Fortunato wore a _____*brightly*_____ colored shirt.
   bright/brightly

2. The bells on Fortunato's hat rang _____ as he walked.
   light/lightly

3. Fortunato had a _____ cough
   terrible/terribly

4. Fortunato turned _____ toward Montressor.
   unsteady/unsteadily

5. Montressor was _____ to attach the chain to a lock.
   quick/quickly

6. Masons are members of a _____ society.
   secret/secretly

Extension Activity

Carnival Hats and Masks

In "The Cask of Amontillado," Fortunato is wearing a hat with little bells on it. Montressor wears a black silk mask.

A. Read about Carnival hats and masks.

During Carnival, people wear costumes that include beautiful masks and wild hats. These masks and hats are made out of many different materials, including felt, velvet, feathers, sequins, and bells.

B. Design a Carnival hat or mask.

- Find pictures of Carnival costumes in an encyclopedia or on the Internet.

- Make photocopies, printouts, or drawings of hats or masks that you like. These will give you ideas for the hat or mask you will make.

- Make your own hat or mask. Use materials such as felt, feathers, construction paper, markers, tape, glue, glitter, and string.

- Wear the hat or mask to a Carnival celebration in your classroom.

Writing Practice

Write an Opinion

When you write your opinion, you tell your thoughts or feelings about a subject. Here is some information about opinions:

An opinion is not a fact.

An opinion cannot be proved.

An opinion can be supported by facts or details.

Read the question below. Then read one student's response to it.

Question: What might Fortunato have done to make Montressor want revenge? Give reasons to support your opinion.

Opinion: *I think Fortunato did many things to make Montressor and his whole family look bad. In the first sentence, Montressor talks about the "thousand injuries of Fortunato" and that Fortunato has "dared to insult" him. Then, in the vaults, Fortunato drinks wine with a nasty smile and says, "I drink to the members of your fine family who are buried in these vaults." He obviously means the opposite. He has no respect for Montressor and his family, and this must be a deep insult for Montressor.*

Write your own opinion in response to one of the questions below. Give at least two reasons to support your opinion.

1. Do you think Montressor is mad (insane)? Why or why not?

2. Do you think "The Cask of Amontillado" is a good story? Why or why not?

3. Do you think this story is realistic? Why or why not?

April Showers

Adapted from the story by Edith Wharton

About the Author

Edith Newbold Jones Wharton was born in New York City in 1862. Her family was wealthy. She read widely and traveled to Europe at an early age. In 1885, she married Teddy Wharton, but the marriage was not happy. In 1913, they were divorced—an unusual, even shocking event at that time. By 1907, Wharton had moved to Paris and resumed the writing she had begun as a teenager. *The House of Mirth* (1905) was her first famous novel. This, like most of her writing, explores the false moral values of upper-class New York society. In 1921, she became the first woman to win the Pulitzer Prize for her novel *The Age of Innocence*. Wharton examines the weaknesses of her characters as if from a distance. Yet the humor and understanding with which she presents her characters encourages us to feel sympathy with them. Wharton died in France in 1937.

Before You Read

About "April Showers"

Characters
Theodora, a seventeen-year-old girl; Uncle James, Theodora's uncle; Kathleen Kyd, a famous novelist; Theodora's family: Mother, Father, Kate, Bertha, Johnny; editor at *Home Circle* magazine

Plot
Theodora has dreams of becoming a great author. Sometimes her dreams interfere with her responsibilities to her family. Theodora completes a novel and sends it to *Home Circle* magazine. She can hardly eat or sleep as she waits to hear from the editor.

Setting
Time: early 1900s
Place: Theodora's home outside of Boston

Theme
An important part of growing up is being brave enough to follow your dreams.

Build Background

An Editor's Job
An editor is someone who decides whether or not to publish a manuscript. Then the same editor, or another editor, helps to get the manuscript ready for publishing. The editor looks for errors and problems in the writing. The editor makes sure that the writing makes sense. He or she checks facts to make sure they are correct. The editor checks for errors in grammar. Editors often correct the mistakes, but sometimes they ask the writer to make the corrections.

Would you rather be a writer or an editor? Why?

Key Words

Read these sentences. Try to understand each word in boldfaced type by looking at the other words in the sentence. Use a dictionary to check your ideas. Write each word and its meaning in your notebook.

1. Edith Wharton wrote many books. She is the **author** of this short story.

2. An **editor** will check an author's writing for errors.

3. Editors usually enjoy reading all kinds of **literature,** that is, any writing that is well written.

4. Today, an author will usually make several copies of his or her written work, the **manuscript.**

5. Edith Wharton's **publisher,** either a person or a company, prepared her manuscript for printing.

6. Some editors love reading **romance** stories because they like reading about characters who are in love.

7. Romance stories are usually **sentimental.** They try to make us cry with happiness or sweet sadness.

Reading Strategy

Identify with a Character

Identifying with a character can help you enjoy and understand what you read. As you read, ask yourself these questions:

- In what ways is the main character like me?

- What would I do if I were in her place?

- How would I feel if I had done what she did?

April Showers

Adapted from the story by Edith Wharton

But Guy's heart slept under the violets on Muriel's grave.

Theodora thought it was a beautiful ending. She had seen girls cry over last chapters that weren't half as sad as this one. She laid her pen aside and read the words again. Then, breathing deeply, she wrote across the bottom of the page the name she would use in literature—Gladys Glyn.

Downstairs the clock struck two. Two o'clock in the morning! And Theodora had promised her mother to be up early to sew buttons on Johnny's jacket, and to make sure that Kate and Bertha took their cod-liver oil[1] before school!

Slowly, tenderly, she gathered up the pages of her manuscript. There were five hundred of them. She tied them together with a blue satin ribbon. Her Aunt Julia had given the ribbon to her. She had wanted to wear it with her new white dress on Sunday. But this was a much nobler use for it. She tied the ends of the ribbon in a pretty bow. Theodora was clever at making bows. She could have been good at decorating things, but she gave all her spare time to literature. Then, with a last look at the precious pages, she closed and addressed the package. She would send it off next morning to *Home Circle*. She knew it would be hard to get published in this magazine, with all its popular authors. But she had been encouraged to try by her Uncle James.

Uncle James had been visiting from Boston, to tell them about his new house. "And who do you think is our new neighbor?" He smiled at Theodora. "Probably you know all about her. Ever hear of Kathleen Kyd?"

Kathleen Kyd! she thought with admiration. The famous novelist, author of more popular romances than all the other

---

[1] *cod-liver oil:* an early source of vitamins, made from cod fish liver

authors put together! The author of *Fashion and Passion, An American Duchess,* and *Rhona's Revolt*! Was there an intelligent girl from Maine to California whose heart would not beat faster at the sound of that name?

"Why, yes," Uncle James was saying. "Kathleen Kyd lives next door. Frances G. Wallop is her real name, and her husband's a dentist. She's a very pleasant kind of woman—you'd never know she was a writer. Ever hear how she began to write? She told me the whole story. It seems she was a saleswoman in a store, earning practically nothing. She had to support her mother and her sister, who's helplessly handicapped. Well, she wrote a story one day, just for fun, and sent it to *Home Circle.* They'd never heard of her, of course, and she never expected to hear from them. She did, though. They took her story and asked for more. She became a regular contributor. Now she tells me her books bring her in about ten thousand dollars[2] a year." He smiled ironically at Theodora's father. "That's rather more than you or I make, eh, John? I certainly hope *this* household doesn't contribute to her support." He looked sharply at Theodora. "I don't believe in feeding young people on sentimental romances!"

Theodora listened breathlessly. Kathleen Kyd's first story had been accepted by *Home Circle* and they had asked for more. Why should Gladys Glyn be less fortunate? Theodora had done a lot of romance reading—far more than her parents were aware of. She felt she could judge the quality of her own work. She was almost sure that her novel, *April Showers,* was a fine book. Perhaps it lacked Kathleen Kyd's tender humor. But it had an emotional depth that Kyd never reached. Theodora did not care to amuse her readers— she would leave that to less serious authors. Her aim was to stir the depths of human emotion,[3] and she felt she had succeeded. It was a great thing for a girl to feel that about her first novel. Theodora was only seventeen—she remembered with a touch of pity that the great author George Eliot[4] had not become famous until she was nearly forty.

[2]*ten thousand dollars:* a very large amount of money at that time
[3]*stir the depths of human emotion:* cause to experience human emotions deeply
[4]*George Eliot:* a novelist, Mary Ann Evans, who wrote using a man's name

April Showers   **31**

No, there was no doubt that *April Showers* was a fine novel. But would a less fine book have a better chance to be published? Would it be wiser to write the book down to the average reader's level, and save for a future novel the great emotion that she had written into this book? No! Never would she change her words to suit ignorant taste! The great authors never sank to such tricks—nor would she. The manuscript should be sent as it was.

Theodora woke up suddenly, worried. What was it? *Home Circle* had refused *April Showers*? No, that couldn't be it. There lay the precious manuscript, waiting to be mailed. Ah, it was the clock downstairs, striking nine o'clock. It was Johnny's buttons, and the girls to get ready!

Theodora jumped out of bed feeling guilty. She didn't want to disappoint her mother about the buttons. Her mother was handicapped by rheumatism,[5] and had to give much of the care of the household to her oldest daughter. Theodora honestly meant to see that Johnny had all his buttons sewed back on, and that Kate and Bertha went to school tidy. Unfortunately, the writing of a great novel leaves little time or memory for the small responsibilities. Theodora usually found that her good intentions came too late for practical results.

Her guilt was softened by the thought that literary success would make up for all her little failings. She intended to spend all her money on her family. Already she could see the wheelchair she would buy for her mother, and the fresh wallpaper for her father's office. She would buy bicycles for the girls, and send Johnny to a boarding school where someone else would sew on his buttons. If her parents could have guessed her intentions, they would not blame her for her failings. And her father, on this particular morning, would not have looked up to say, in his weary, ironic way, "I suppose you didn't get home from the dance till morning?"

Theodora's sense of good intentions helped her take her father's criticism calmly. "I'm sorry to be late, father," she said. Her

[5]*rheumatism* (ROO-muh-tizm): stiff, painful joints or muscles

tenderness would have quieted a parent in fiction, but Dr. Dace never behaved like a father in a book.

"Your apology shows your good manners," he said impatiently, "but manners won't keep your mother's breakfast warm."

"Hasn't mother's tray gone up yet?"

"Who was to take it, I'd like to know? The girls came down so late that I had to hurry them off before they'd finished breakfast. And Johnny's hands were so dirty that I sent him back to his room to clean up. It's a fine thing when the doctor's children are the dirtiest children in town!"

Theodora quickly prepared her mother's tray, leaving her own breakfast untouched. As she entered the room upstairs her mother smiled tenderly at her. But Mrs. Dace's patience was harder to bear than Dr. Dace's criticism.

"Mother, I'm *so* sorry—"

"No matter, dear. I suppose Johnny's buttons kept you. I can't think what that boy does to his clothes!"

Theodora set the tray down without answering. She couldn't talk about her forgetfulness without giving away the cause of it. For a few weeks longer she would have to be misunderstood. Then—ah, then, if her novel was accepted, how gladly she would forget and forgive misunderstanding! But what if it were refused? She turned away from her mother to hide her worry. Well, if it was refused, she would ask her parents to forgive *her*. She would settle down without complaining to a wasted life of sewing and cod-liver oil.

Theodora had said to herself that after the manuscript had been sent off, she would have time to look after the children. But she hadn't thought about the mailman. He came three times a day. For an hour before each visit, she was too excited to work, wondering if he would bring an answer this time. And for an hour after he left she moved about in a heavy cloud of disappointment. Meanwhile, the children had never been so difficult. They seemed always to be coming to pieces like cheap furniture. Mrs. Dace worried herself ill over Johnny's clothes, Bertha's bad marks at school, and Kate's

refusal to take her cod-liver oil. And Dr. Dace came home late from visiting his patients to find a cold fireplace and nothing to eat. He called angrily for Theodora to come downstairs and take the embroidered[6] words, "East, West, Home Is Best" down off the wall.

The week was a long nightmare. Theodora could neither eat nor sleep. She was up early enough. But instead of taking care of the children and making breakfast, she wandered down the street to meet the mailman. Then she would come back empty-handed, forgetting her morning responsibilities. She had no idea how long she would be forced to wait, but she didn't see how authors could live if they were kept waiting more than a week.

Then, suddenly, one evening—she never knew how or when it happened—she found herself with a *Home Circle* envelope in her hand. Her eyes flashed over the letter—a wild dance of words that wouldn't settle down and make sense.

"Dear Madam:" (They called her Madam!) And then, yes, the words were beginning to fall into line now. "Your novel, *April Showers*, has been received, and we are glad to accept it on the usual terms. Chapters of a novel we were planning to start publishing were delayed due to the author's illness. The first chapter of *April Showers* will therefore appear in our midsummer edition. Thanking you for sending this contribution, Sincerely yours . . ." and so forth.

Theodora ran outside into the spring evening. Spring! Everything was crowding toward the light, and in her own heart, hundreds of hopes burst into leaf. She looked up through the trees at the tender moon. She felt surrounded by an atmosphere of loving understanding. The brown earth was full of joy. The treetops moved with joy. A joyous star burst through the branches, as if to say, "I know!"

Theodora, on the whole, behaved very well. Her mother cried, her father whistled, and said (but less ironically than usual) that he supposed he'd never get a hot meal again. And the children added noisily to this unfamiliar, joyous scene.

[6]*embroidered:* sewn with decorative colored thread

Within a week, everybody in town knew that Theodora had written a novel, and that it was coming out in *Home Circle*. Other girls copied her way of dressing and speaking. The local newspaper asked her for a poem. Her old school teachers stopped to shake her hand, and shyly congratulated her. Uncle James even came down from Boston to talk about her success. From what Kathleen Kyd told him, he thought Theodora would probably get a thousand dollars for her story. He suggested that she should give him the money to buy shares in a company he was interested in, and suggested a plot for her next romance.

Theodora waited impatiently for the midsummer *Home Circle*— and at last the great day came. Before the bookstore opened, Theodora was waiting on the sidewalk to buy the midsummer *Home Circle*. She ran home without opening the precious magazine. Her excitement was almost more than she could bear. Not hearing her father call her to breakfast, she ran upstairs and locked herself in her room. Her hands shook so that she could hardly turn the pages. At last—yes, there it was: *April Showers*.

The magazine dropped from her hands. What name had she read beneath the title? Had her emotion blinded her?

"*April Showers*, by Kathleen Kyd"

Kathleen Kyd! Oh, cruel misprint! Oh, careless editor! Through tears of furious disappointment, Theodora looked again. Yes, she had made no mistake—it was that hateful name. She found herself reading a paragraph that she had never seen before. She read farther. It was all strange. The truth burst upon her: *it was not her story*!

It was hours later. Theodora never knew how she had got back to the Boston train station. She had struggled through the crowd, and was pushed into the train. It would be dark when she got home, but that didn't matter. Nothing mattered now. She sank into her seat, and closed her eyes. She tried to shut out what had happened in the last few hours, but minute by minute her memory forced her to relive the experience.

Although she didn't know Boston well, she had made her way easily enough to the *Home Circle* building. At least, she supposed she had. She remembered nothing until she found herself going up the stairs as easily as one does unbelievable things in dreams. She must have been walking fast, for her heart was beating furiously. She barely had breath to whisper the editor's name to the young man who met her. He led her to an inner office which seemed filled by a huge force. Theodora felt herself overpowered, conquered by this force—she could hardly speak or hear.

Gradually, words floated up around her. "*April Showers*, Mrs. Kyd's new novel? Your manuscript, you say? You have a letter from me? The name, please? It must be some unfortunate misunderstanding. One moment." And then a bell was ringing, the young man was unlocking a cupboard, and the manuscript, her own precious manuscript, tied with Aunt Julia's ribbon, was laid on the table before her. Her stream of angry questions was drowned in a flood of pleasant apology: "An unfortunate accident—Mrs. Kyd's manuscript received the same day—how strange you chose the same title—two acceptance letters sent by mistake—Miss Dace's novel didn't suit their needs—should, of course, have been returned—so sorry—accidents would happen—sure she understood—."

The voice went on. When it stopped, Theodora found herself in the street. A taxi nearly ran her over. A car honked in her ears. She held her manuscript tenderly in the crowd, like a live thing that had been hurt. She could not bear to look at its soiled edges, and the ink spot on Aunt Julia's ribbon.

The train stopped suddenly. It was her stop. She saw other passengers getting off and she followed them into the darkness. A warm wind blew into her face the smell of summer woods. She thought back to the spring when she had been so full of joy. Then she thought of home. She had run out in the morning without a word. Her heart sank at the thought of her mother's fears. And her father—how angry he would be! She bent her head under the coming storm of his criticism.

The night was cloudy, and as she stepped into the darkness a hand was slipped into hers. She stood still, too weary to feel frightened. A voice said, quietly:

◆

"Don't walk so fast, child. You look tired."

"Father! You were at the station?" she whispered.

"It's such a good night, I thought I'd wander down and meet you."

She could not see his face in the darkness, but the light of his cigar looked down on her like a friendly eye. She took courage to say, "Then you knew—"

"That you'd gone to Boston? Well, I thought you probably had."

They walked on slowly, and then he added, "You see, you left the *Home Circle* lying in your room."

How she blessed the dark sky! She couldn't have borne even the tiniest star to look at her. "Then Mother wasn't much frightened?"

"Why, no, she didn't seem to be. She's been busy all day over some sewing for Bertha."

Theodora's voice was choked with tears. "Father, I'll—" She reached for words, but they escaped her. "I'll do things—differently; I haven't meant—" Suddenly she heard herself bursting out: "It was all a mistake, you know—about my story. They didn't want it; they won't have it!" She couldn't bear his amusement.

She felt his arm around her, and was sure he was laughing. But they moved on in silence. Then he said:

"It hurts a bit just at first, doesn't it?"

"Oh, Father!"

He stood still a moment, and the light of his cigar shone on his face. "You see, I've been through it myself."

"You, Father? You?"

"Why, yes. Didn't I ever tell you? I wrote a novel once. I was just out of college, and didn't want to be a doctor. No; I wanted to be a brilliant writer. So I wrote a novel."

The doctor paused, and Theodora held fast to his arm in silent sympathy. It was as if a drowning creature caught a live hand in the murderous fury of the waves.

"It took me a year—a whole year's hard work. When I'd finished, no publisher would have it, not at any price. That's why I came to meet you, because I remembered my walk home." ✑

After You Read

Understand the Story

Answer these questions in your notebook. Write complete sentences.

1. Who, or what, was Gladys Glyn?
   a writer

2. Who was Kathleen Kyd? What was her real name?
   Gladys Glyn

3. Where did Theodora send her manuscript?
   to the "Home circle."

4. How did Theodora's family, her teachers, and others behave toward her when they heard that her manuscript had been accepted? *feel happy for her*

5. What did Theodora discover when she read the midsummer *Home Circle*? *It's not her book*

6. What did she find out when she got to Boston?
   Something is worry

7. How did Theodora's father react to her misfortune?
   He try to be a writer before

Elements of Literature

Metaphor

A **metaphor** is a comparison of two things that are not like each other. Here is an example: "My love is a red, red rose." In this metaphor, love is being compared with a red rose. The following metaphor is from the story you just read:

> Her eyes flashed over the letter—a wild dance of words that wouldn't settle down and make sense.

In this metaphor, the letter is compared with a wild dance. Here is another example from "April Showers":

> Her stream of angry questions was drowned in a flood of pleasant apology. . . .

In this example, two sets of things are being compared. In one part of the sentence, angry questions are being compared with a stream. What two things are being compared in the other part of the sentence?

Discussion

Discuss in pairs or small groups.

1. What do you think of Theodora? Do you like her and feel sympathy for her? Or do you think she was silly to believe she could be a famous writer?

2. What do you think of Theodora's father, Dr. Dace? What does he expect of Theodora? Are his expectations fair? Were you surprised by his behavior at the end of the story? Why or why not?

Vocabulary

Choose the correct word. Write the completed sentences in your notebook.

1. Theodora gave all her spare time to ___A___.
   a. sewing   **b.** decorating   **c.** literature

2. Theodora gathered up the five hundred pages of her __C__ and tied them together with a blue satin ribbon.
   a. author   **b.** manuscript   **c.** magazine

3. Kathleen Kyd was the author of more popular __B__ than all the other authors put together!
   a. romances   **b.** editors   **c.** publishers

4. Uncle James didn't believe that young people should read __C__ romances.
   a. neighbor   **b.** sentimental   **c.** literature

5. George Eliot was a famous __A__.
   a. author   **b.** editor   **c.** dentist

6. Theodora whispered the name of the __B__ to the man.
   a. literature   **b.** doctor   **c.** editor

7. No __C__ wanted Dr. Dace's novel, not at any price.
   a. publisher   **b.** romance   **c.** manuscript

Word Study

Write the sentences below in your notebook. Complete each sentence with the correct form of the word. Use the chart to help you. The first one has been done for you.

Verb	Adjective
criticize	critical
congratulate	congratulatory
intend	intentional
complain	complaining
apologize	apologetic

1. Dr. Dace is _____critical_____ of Theodora's behavior.
   criticize/critical

2. Theodora is excited to receive the _____ letter
   congratulate/congratulatory
   from *Home Circle*.

3. It turns out that *Home Circle* did not _____ to
   intend/intentional
   publish Theodora's story after all.

4. Theodora promises herself that she will not _____
   complain/complaining
   about helping with the children if her book is refused.

5. The editor of *Home Circle* is _____ about the mistake.
   apologize/apologetic

42

Extension Activity

Be a Critic

When a new short-story collection is first published in a book, it may be reviewed. People who review the stories are called reviewers, or critics.

A. Read a review that might have been written by a story critic who read "April Showers" by Edith Wharton.

> Edith Wharton engages the reader in a wonderful story of a young woman who dreams of becoming a great author. The time is the early 1900s. When we meet Theodora, she is just about to send off her first manuscript to *Home Circle* magazine. As the story continues, we feel Theodora's suspense as she waits for a response from the editor. Will her story be accepted? Wharton gives the reader a surprise at the end of this realistic story.

B. Choose a short story that you have read in this book or in another book. Be a story critic. Answer these questions and discuss them with a partner.

1. What is the title of the story?

2. Who are the main characters?

3. What is the story's setting?

4. What happens to the main character?

5. Which of these words describe the story?

wonderful
unusual
dull
interesting
clever
uninteresting

Writing Practice

Plan a Story

A **story** is a short work of fiction. A story usually has a clear beginning, middle, and end. The writer's purpose is to entertain or inform the reader. A story usually includes the following:

- Characters—the people in a story

- Setting—the story's time and place

- Plot—a series of events that include a problem or conflict

- Theme—the message the writer wants the reader to understand

Think about an experience you had that would make a good story. Decide on the message you want to give your reader. Then copy and fill in the following story outline.

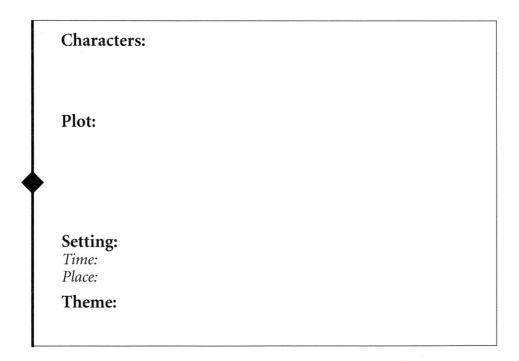

Characters:

Plot:

Setting:
Time:
Place:
Theme:

3

Rip Van Winkle

Adapted from the story by Washington Irving

About the Author

Washington Irving was the first widely read American writer of short stories. He was born in 1783 in New York City. Irving was a lively child who was so bored by school that he stopped formal studies at the age of sixteen. In 1809, he published *A History of New York, by Dietrich Knickerbocker,* a humorous book that had great success. Irving was not yet ready for a literary career, however, and so he joined his brother's business. In 1815, he went to live in Europe to represent the family company. When the business failed, Irving started writing seriously for a living. In 1819, he published *A Sketch Book,* which includes the story "Rip Van Winkle." One of Irving's last works was *The Life of Washington,* which he considered his finest book. Soon after completing it, in 1859, he died at Sunnyside—his home on the Hudson River in New York State.

Before You Read

About "Rip Van Winkle"

Characters
Rip Van Winkle, a poor farmer; Dame Van Winkle, his wife; a stranger; Peter Vanderdonk, oldest man in the village; Judith Gardenier, Rip Van Winkle's daughter

Plot
Rip Van Winkle is a fun-loving character with little interest in work. Everyone likes him, except his wife. She complains constantly about his laziness. One day, Rip Van Winkle goes for a long walk. What happens to him makes an amazing and wonderful story.

Setting
Time: a time before 1775; a time after 1781
Place: a Dutch colony in the Catskill Mountains

Theme
Time changes everything, except the past.

Build Background

The American Revolution

This story takes place before and after the American Revolution. Before this war, thirteen colonies in America belonged to England. In 1776, the Declaration of Independence was written. It explained why it was necessary for the colonies to gain their independence from King George III of England. To gain their independence, the Americans fought against the British. The war, called the American Revolution or the Revolutionary War, lasted from 1775 to 1781. Led by General George Washington, the Americans won their independence.

George Washington is an American hero. With a partner, talk about a hero from your home country.

Key Words

Read these sentences. Try to understand each word in boldfaced type by looking at the other words in the sentence. Use a dictionary to check your ideas. Write each word and its meaning in your notebook.

1. This **colony** was a place that had been settled by a group of people from Holland.

2. Rip's wife was called **Dame** Van Winkle, which is an old way of saying Mrs. Van Winkle.

3. **Dutch** people, who were from Holland, came to America to find freedom.

4. The **henpecked** husband listened to the constant complaining of his wife and did nothing about it.

5. Rip's **shrewish** wife was unkind and spent her time complaining to her husband.

Reading Strategy

Look for Causes and Effects

Looking for causes and effects as you read can help you understand a story better. A short story is made up of events. The event (what happens) is an **effect.** Why the event happens is the **cause.**

Here is an example from the story you are about to read:

> **Cause:** Rip Van Winkle found it impossible to do his family duty or to keep his farm in order.

> **Effect:** Rip's own poor farm—the falling-down fences, the wandering cow, the bare field—was the worst in the village.

As you read, look for causes and effects.

Rip Van Winkle

Adapted from the story by Washington Irving

Whoever has made a voyage up the Hudson River must remember the Catskill Mountains. They are seen away to the west of the river, rising up to a noble height. Every change of season, every change of weather, indeed every hour of the day, produces some change in their magical colors and shapes.

At the foot of these mountains the voyager may have noticed the light smoke curving upwards from a village set among the trees. It is a little village of great age. It was built by Dutch colonists in early times. The houses were made of small yellow bricks brought from Holland, and they were built in the old style of Dutch country houses.

In that same village, and in one of those very houses (which to tell the exact truth was sadly time-worn and weather-beaten), there lived a simple good-natured fellow named Rip Van Winkle. This was many years ago, when the country was still a colony of Great Britain. Even before that, the Van Winkle family had served bravely in the army of the Dutch Governor, Peter Stuyvesant. Rip, however, was not blessed with his family's war-like character. I have said that he was a simple good-natured fellow; he was moreover a kind neighbor and an obedient, henpecked husband. Indeed, the mildness of spirit that made him so popular in his village may have come from being so henpecked in his house. After all, consider the men who are sweet, easy, and willing to please in the world; they are often those who are under the control of a sharp-tongued shrew at home. By causing this sweetness in her husband, a shrewish wife may in some ways be considered a reasonable blessing—and if so, Rip Van Winkle was thoroughly blessed.

It is certain that he was a great favorite among all the good wives of the village. They always took his side in family quarrels and lay all the blame on Dame Van Winkle. The children of the village, too, would shout with joy whenever he approached. He taught them games, made their playthings, and told them long stories of ghosts and devils and Indians. The children followed him all over the village, hanging on his coat and playing tricks on him. And not a dog would bark at him throughout the village.

The great weakness in Rip's character was a powerful dislike of all kinds of profitable work. This laziness could not be from a lack of patience or energy. He could sit on a wet rock and fish all day without a single complaint. He could carry a heavy gun on his shoulder for hours, walking through woods and up hills, to shoot a few rabbits or wild birds. He would never refuse to help a neighbor with the roughest work. And he was the best man for preparing Indian corn at all country parties, or for building stone fences, or for doing little jobs for the women of the village that their husbands wouldn't do. In a word, Rip was ready to pay attention to anybody's business but his own. To do his family duty or to keep his farm in order—he found these things impossible. His own poor farm—the falling-down fences, the wandering cow, the bare field—was the worst in the village. His son and daughter were poorly dressed and wild. They, and Rip's dog, Wolf, looked like they belonged to nobody.

Rip Van Winkle, however, was one of those happy men of foolish, easygoing natures who take the world lightly, eat white bread or brown, and would rather go hungry on a penny than work for a dollar. Alone, Rip would have whistled life away in perfect happiness. But his wife kept shouting in his ears about his laziness, his carelessness, and the ruin he was bringing on his family. Morning, noon, and night, her tongue was going non-stop. Everything Rip did produced a flood of shrewish talk. Rip's only reply to these angry speeches was to lift his shoulders, shake his head, roll his eyes, and go outside of the house—the only side which, in truth, belongs to the henpecked husband.

Times grew worse and worse with Rip Van Winkle as the years of marriage went by; a bitter heart never sweetens with age, and a tongue is the only edged tool that grows sharper with frequent use. Forced from home, Rip often found pleasure in a kind of club of wise men, philosophers, and other non-working men of the village. They held their meetings under a great tree in front of the village inn, which travelers knew by its sign, a painted picture of King George the Third of England. Here the club's members used to sit in the shade through a long, lazy summer's day, talking of village matters, or telling endless, sleepy stories about nothing. Derrick Van Bummel, the well-dressed little schoolmaster, would sometimes read to them from an old newspaper. They would discuss with great seriousness events that had taken place some months before. These discussions were guided by the innkeeper, Nicholas Vedder, and his pipe. He never spoke a word, but when he disagreed with an opinion, black smoke came in quantity from the pipe, and when he agreed, he removed the pipe from his mouth and let the smoke curl sweetly about his nose.

Even from this favorite hiding place, however, Rip was chased by his wife. She would break in on the peaceful club meetings and direct her anger at all the club's members for encouraging laziness in her husband. In the end, poor Rip found only one way to escape the labor of the farm and the anger of Dame Van Winkle. This was to take gun in hand and walk away into the woods. He would sometimes sit at the foot of a tree and share his simple meal with Wolf, whom he saw as a fellow-sufferer. "Poor Wolf," he would say, "your lady leads you a dog's life; but never mind, my boy, while I live you will never lack a friend to stand by you!" The dog would wag his tail and look sadly in his master's face; and if dogs can feel pity, I do believe he returned the feeling with all his heart.

On one of these wanderings on a fine autumn day, Rip had unknowingly climbed to one of the highest parts of the Catskill Mountains. He was hunting rabbits, and the stillness of the woodlands had echoed and re-echoed with the sound of his gun. Tired and out of breath, he threw himself, late in the afternoon, on a small round green hill covered with mountain bushes. From an opening between the trees he could overlook all the lower country with its miles of rich woodland. He saw at a distance the lordly Hudson River, far, far below him, moving on its silent but noble course. On the other side he looked down into a deep mountain valley, wild and lonely, the bottom filled with rocks that had fallen from the high hills above. Evening was approaching. The mountains began to throw their long blue shadows over the valleys. He saw that it would be dark before he could reach the village, and he sighed heavily when he thought of being met with the terrors of Dame Van Winkle.

As he was about to descend, he heard a voice from a distance, shouting, "Rip Van Winkle! Rip Van Winkle!" He looked round, but could see nothing but a blackbird flying its lonely way across the mountain. He thought his imagination must have tricked him, and turned again to descend, when he heard the same cry through the still evening air: "Rip Van Winkle! Rip Van Winkle!" Wolf made a low noise in his throat and drew nearer to his master's side, looking fearfully down the valley. Rip now felt a strong uncertainty coming over him. He looked anxiously in the same direction, and saw a strange figure working its way up the rocks, and bending under the weight of something he carried on his back. Rip was surprised to see any human being in this lonely place, but thinking it might be one of the villagers in need of his help, he hurried down to give it.

As he approached he was still more surprised by the stranger's appearance. He was a short, square-built old fellow, with thick bushy hair and a beard. He was dressed in the old Dutch fashion—a short cloth coat belted at the waist and broad trousers gathered at the knees. He carried on his back a heavy barrel, the kind that holds beer or whiskey, and he made signs for Rip to approach and help with his load. Though rather shy and distrustful of the stranger, Rip gave help with his usual speed. Helping each other, they climbed up the dry bed of a mountain stream. As they climbed, Rip heard long,

deep rolling sounds, like distant thunder. The sound seemed to come out of an opening in the hill above them. He stopped briefly, but decided that it was only a mountain thunder-shower, and continued to climb. Passing through the opening in the hill, the two men came into a round open space, an amphitheater. It was surrounded by high hills with tall trees on their tops, so you could see little of the darkening sky or the bright evening cloud. During the whole time Rip and the stranger had climbed in silence. Although Rip wondered greatly at the purpose of carrying a barrel of strong drink up this wild mountain, there was something strange about the unknown that kept him silent.

On entering the amphitheater, he was greeted by still more unusual sights. On a level spot in the center was a company of odd-looking fellows playing at nine-pins, slowly rolling the balls at the wooden pins. Some of the men wore jackets, others wore short coats, with knives in their belts. Most of them wore broad trousers like Rip's guide. Their whole appearance was strange. One had a large head, broad face, and small piggish eyes. Another's face seemed to consist mostly of nose, and was topped by a pointed white hat with a red feather in it. There was one who seemed to be the commander. He was a fat old gentleman, with a weather-beaten face. He wore a formal black jacket, a broad belt and sword, red stockings, and high-heeled shoes with roses on them. The whole group reminded Rip of the figures in an old Dutch painting he had seen in the house of Dominic Van Shaick, the village minister, and which had been brought over from Holland when the colony was first settled.

What seemed especially odd to Rip was the way these folks played at their game of nine-pins. They kept the most serious faces as they played, and the most mysterious silence. The only sound was that of the balls hitting the wooden pins and echoing along the mountains like rolling thunder.

As Rip and his companion approached them, they suddenly stopped their play. They looked straight at him with such statue-like faces that his heart turned within him, and his knees knocked together. His companion now emptied the contents of the barrel into large drinking cups, and made signs for him to serve the company. He obeyed, shaking with fear. The men drank in the deepest silence, and then returned to their game.

Gradually, Rip's anxiety lessened. He even dared, when no eye was fixed upon him, to taste the drink, which he thought had much the flavor of a fine Holland whiskey. He was naturally a thirsty fellow, and soon allowed himself a second drink. One taste led to another, and he repeated his visits to the drinking cup so often that finally his senses were overpowered. His eyes swam in his head, his head gradually dropped to his chest, and he fell into a deep sleep.

When he awoke, he found himself on the small round green hill where he had first seen his companion, the old man of the valley. He rubbed his eyes—it was a bright sunny morning. The birds were jumping and singing in the bushes. "Surely," thought Rip, "I have not slept here all night?" He remembered what had happened before he fell asleep. The strange man with the barrel—the climb up the dry stream-bed—the amphitheater among the rocks—the strange serious party at nine-pins—the drinking cup. "Oh! That cup! That evil cup!" thought Rip. "What excuse shall I make to Dame Van Winkle?"

He looked round for his gun, but in place of the clean well-oiled weapon, he found an old gun, its iron time-worn and its wood worm-eaten. He now suspected that the serious games-players of the mountain had tricked him with strong drink and stolen his gun. Wolf, too, had disappeared, though he might have gone after rabbits or birds. He whistled for him and called his name, but no dog came.

He decided to revisit the scene of last night's events, and if he met with any of the group, to demand his gun and his dog. As he rose to walk, he felt an unusual tightness in his legs, arms, and all his body. "These mountain beds do not agree with me," thought Rip. He descended again into the deep valley. He found the dry stream-bed which he and his companion had climbed up the evening before. But to his great surprise a mountain stream was now rushing down it, leaping from rock to rock and filling the valley with its pleasant sound. With difficulty he climbed up its sides, fighting his way through thick bushes and the branches of small trees.

Finally, he came to the place where an opening had led through the hill to the amphitheater; but no signs of such an opening remained. Only high rocks greeted him, and the stream that flowed quickly over them. Here, then, poor Rip was brought to a stop. He called again and whistled for his dog; he was answered only by the blackbirds flying high in the trees above him. What could he do? The morning was passing away, and he was very hungry. He shook his head, shouldered the old gun, and turned his steps toward home.

As he approached the village, he met a number of people, but he knew none of them. This surprised him, for he had thought he knew everyone in the country around. Their clothes, too, were in a fashion different from the one he knew. They looked equally surprised to meet him. Many of them brought their hands to their chins when they saw him, and when Rip copied the movement he found, to his surprise, that his beard had grown a foot long!

He had now entered the village. A group of strange children ran at his heels, shouting after him and pointing at his long gray beard. The dogs barked as he passed. The village itself was changed; it was larger, with many more people. There were rows of houses he had never seen before. Strange names were over the doors—strange faces at the windows—everything was strange. He began to wonder whether some kind of magic was at work. Surely this was his own village, which he had left just the day before. There stood the Catskill Mountains; there was the silver Hudson at a distance. Rip was very confused. "That cup last night," thought he, "has mixed up my brain thoroughly!"

It was with some difficulty that he found the way to his own house, which he approached with some fear, expecting every moment to hear the angry voice of Dame Van Winkle. But he found the house in ruins—the roof fallen in, the windows broken, the doors hanging off. He entered the house, which, to tell the truth, Dame Van Winkle had always kept in neat order. It was a sad, empty shell. Frightened, he called loudly for his wife and children. The lonely rooms rang for a moment with his voice, and then all again was silence.

He now hurried away toward his club's old meeting place at the village's small inn—but it too was gone. In its place stood a large ugly wooden building with the word HOTEL above the door. Instead of the great tree in front of it, there was a tall wooden pole, and from it hung a flag with a strange pattern of stars and stripes in red, white, and blue. He saw the inn's old sign, but even this was changed. King George's round face was the same, but his red coat was changed to one of blue. Instead of a crown, he wore a hat and held a sword. And underneath the picture, in large letters, was painted:

GENERAL WASHINGTON

There was, as usual, a crowd of folk near the door, but no one that Rip remembered. He looked for wise old Nicholas Vedder with his pipe, or the little schoolmaster Van Bummel, reading from an old newspaper. In place of these men, a thin, nervous-looking fellow was shouting a speech to the crowd about government—freedom—citizens—elections—heroes of the revolutionary war—and other words completely unknown to the confused Van Winkle.

The appearance of Rip, with his long beard, old gun, strange clothes, and an army of women and children at his heels, attracted the attention of the politicians in the crowd. They gathered round him, eyeing him from head to foot with great curiosity. The thin speech-maker hurried up to him, and bringing him to one side, asked "on which side he voted?" Rip looked at him with complete, empty stupidity. "I say, which political party do you belong to?" the man insisted. Rip had no idea how to answer such a question. Then a knowing, self-important gentleman made his way through the crowd, putting folks to the right and left with his elbows as he passed. He positioned himself before Van Winkle, and demanded in a serious voice "what brought him to the election with a gun on his shoulder and a wild crowd at his heels, and whether he meant to cause trouble in the village?"—"Oh, dear, gentlemen," cried Rip, "I am a poor, quiet man, a native of the place, and a faithful subject of the king, God bless him!"

Here a general shout burst from the bystanders: "A spy! A spy! The enemy! Away with him!" It was with great difficulty that the self-important man brought order again to the crowd. Then, with even deeper seriousness than before, he demanded of the stranger why he had come there, and whom he was searching for? The poor man promised that he meant no harm, but merely came in search of some of his neighbors, who used to meet at the old hotel.

"Well—who are they?—name them."

Rip thought for a moment, then asked, "Where's Nicholas Vedder?"

There was a silence for a while, then an old man replied, in a thin little voice, "Nicholas Vedder! Why, he is dead and gone these eighteen years! There was a wooden marker in the churchyard that used to tell about him, but that's rotten and gone, too."

"Where's Van Bummel, the schoolmaster?"

"Oh, he went off to the army, right at the beginning of the war. He became a famous general, and now he's in the government."

Rip's heart died away at hearing of these sad changes in his home and friends, and finding himself so alone in the world. Every answer puzzled him, too, by mentioning matters he could not understand— eighteen years, and war, and revolution, and government. So when the self-important man finally asked him who he was, he cried out, "God knows! I'm not myself—I'm somebody else—I was myself last night, but I fell asleep on the mountain, and they've changed my

gun, and everything's changed, and I'm changed, and I can't tell
what's my name or who I am!"

The by-standers began now to look at each other, give little
smiles, close one eye, and press their fingers against their foreheads.
At this very moment, a pretty young woman passed through the

crowd to have a look at the gray-bearded man. She had a round little child in her arms who, frightened by the strange old man, began to cry. "Hush, Rip," cried she, "hush, you little fool; the old man won't hurt you." The name of the child, the look of the mother, something in her voice, all awakened memories in his mind. "What is your name, my good woman?" asked he.

"Judith Gardenier."

"And your father's name?"

"Ah, poor man, Rip Van Winkle was his name, but it's twenty years since he went away from home with his gun, and never has been heard of since. His dog came home without him; but whether he shot himself or was carried away by Indians, nobody can tell. I was only a little girl then."

Rip had only one more question to ask; but he said with a shaking voice: "Where's your mother?"

"Oh, she too died, just a short time ago. She had a heart attack while shouting at a traveling salesman."

There was some comfort, at least, in this information. The honest man could no longer control himself. He gathered his daughter and her child in his arms. "I am your father!" he cried. "Young Rip Van Winkle once; old Rip Van Winkle now! Does nobody know poor Rip Van Winkle?"

All stood in silent wonder, until an old woman came out of the crowd, looked closely at his face for a moment, and finally cried, "Sure enough! It is Rip Van Winkle! It is himself! Welcome home again, old neighbor. Why, where have you been these twenty long years?!"

Rip's story was soon told, for the entire twenty years had been to him just as one night. The neighbors at first could not believe it. They shook their heads in doubt, and smiled their smiles at each other. However, they decided to get the opinion of old Peter Vanderdonk, who was seen then slowly advancing up the road. He was descended from the famous historian of that name, who wrote one of the earliest accounts of the region. Peter was the oldest man in the village, and very knowledgeable about all the wonderful events and traditions of the neighborhood. He remembered Rip immediately, and supported his story in the most satisfactory manner. He stated as a historical fact that the Catskill Mountains had always had magical qualities. There was no doubt, he said, that the great Hendrick Hudson, the first discoverer of the river and country, returned every twenty years with the crew of his ship. In this way, Hudson could revisit the scene of his adventures and keep a guardian eye on the river. Vanderdonk's own father had once seen them in their old Dutch clothes playing at nine-pins in a valley of the mountains. And he himself had heard, one summer afternoon, the sound of their balls, like distant rolling thunder.

To make a long story short, the company broke up, and returned to the more important matters of the election. Rip's daughter took him home to live with her. And in time, Rip again began his old walks and habits. He soon found many of his old friends, all of them rather the worse for the wear and tear of time. He preferred the younger people of the village, who grew to like him, too. He could often be found sitting in his old place outside the hotel.

It was some time before he could understand the strange events that had taken place during his sleep: There had been a revolutionary war; the country was no longer a prisoner of old England; and, instead of being a subject of King George the Third of England, he was now a free citizen of the United States of America. Rip, in fact, was no politician. The changes of states and government leaders made little impression on him. To be sure, he understood and was grateful for his freedom—from Dame Van Winkle. Whenever her name was mentioned, however, he only lifted his shoulders, shook his head, and rolled his eyes.

He used to tell his story to every stranger that arrived at the hotel. Some always doubted the reality of it, and insisted that Rip had been out of his head. But nearly all of the old Dutch villagers believed it fully. Even to this day, when they hear a thunderstorm on a summer afternoon in the Catskills, they say that Hendrick Hudson and his crew are at their game of nine-pins. And it is a common wish of all henpecked husbands in the neighborhood, when life hangs heavy on their hands, that they might have a quieting drink out of Rip Van Winkle's cup. ❧

After You Read

Understand the Story

Answer these questions in your notebook. Write complete sentences.

1. Where and when did Rip Van Winkle live?

   Before the revolution war

2. What was the name of Rip's dog?

   Wolf

3. What was the "great weakness" in Rip's character?

   help people and don't care his own family

4. Why did Rip go off into the woods?

   to hunt

5. Where and why did Rip fall asleep?

   in the woods

6. What had happened in the world while Rip slept?

   20 years after.

Elements of Literature

Setting

Read this passage from the beginning of the story. Then answer the questions.

> Whoever has made a voyage up the Hudson River must remember the Catskill Mountains. They are seen away to the west of the river, rising up to a noble height. Every change of season, every change of weather, indeed every hour of the day, produces some change in their magical colors and shapes.

What words does the author use to describe the story's setting? What do you think the author wants you to appreciate about the Catskill Mountains? Explain.

Discussion

Discuss in pairs or small groups.

1. Do you ever want to be asleep instead of doing what you are doing? What kind of activity makes you feel this way? Explain.

2. In Washington Irving's story, Rip Van Winkle sleeps through twenty years of American history that brought far-reaching and sometimes violent change to the country. From what you know about Rip from the story, what events or changes do you think he was happy to miss? What events or changes might he have regretted missing?

Vocabulary

Choose the correct word. Write the completed sentences in your notebook.

1. Rip Van Winkle lived many years ago, when the country was still a ___A___ of Great Britain.
   a. colony   **b.** dame   **c.** Dutch

2. Rip was married to ___B___ Van Winkle.
   a. Dutch   **b.** Dame   **c.** Wolf

3. A ___C___ wife may be considered a reasonable blessing if she causes a sweetness in her husband.
   a. dame   **b.** henpecked   **c.** shrewish

4. The outside of a house is the only side that belongs to a ___B___ husband.
   a. colony   **b.** henpecked   **c.** shrewish

5. The whole group reminded Rip of the figures in an old ___C___ painting that had been brought over from Holland.
   a. Dutch   **b.** Dame   **c.** Colony

Word Study

Look at the chart. Notice that for each verb there are two noun forms. One noun form is an idea or a thing. The other noun form is the person who performs the action of the verb.

Write the sentences below in your notebook. Complete each sentence with the correct form of the word. Use the chart to help you. The first one has been done for you.

Verb	Noun (idea or thing)	Noun (person)
colonize	colony	colonist
frequent	frequency	frequenter
complain	complaint	complainer
philosophize	philosophy	philosopher
discover	discovery	discoverer

1. The Dutch were the first _____colonists_____ in the Hudson River Valley.
   colony/colonists

2. Rip sat in front of the old inn with great _____.
   frequency/frequenter

3. Dame Winkle was a constant _____.
   complaint/complainer

4. They said that Nicholas Vedder was born with a pipe in his mouth and _____ in his blood.
   philosophy/philosopher

5. Hendrick Hudson, the first _____ of the river and
   discovery/discoverer

   country, returned every twenty years with the crew of his ship.

Extension Activity

Hudson River School

The Catskill Mountains inspired Washington Irving to write. Artists were also inspired by the beautiful mountains.

A. Read about the Hudson River School.

In the early 1800s, steamboats brought many visitors to the Catskill Mountains in New York. The region was breathtaking, and many artists went there to paint. One artist who painted scenes along the Hudson River Valley was Thomas Cole. He became a leading American landscape painter. Cole painted dramatic scenes of woods, lakes, waterfalls, and mountains. The group of artists who used a similar style of painting became known as the Hudson River School. Paintings by the artists of the Hudson River School are shown in museums all over the United States.

B. Draw or paint a picture of a beautiful landscape. Follow these steps:

- To get ideas, find pictures of the Hudson River Valley on the Internet or in library books.

- Think about what to include in your landscape. Use pencils to make sketches of your ideas.

- Once you are pleased with a sketch, turn it into a finished work of art. Use colored pencils, pastels, or paints to create your landscape.

- Share your picture with a small group.

Writing Practice

Write a Descriptive Paragraph

A good **descriptive paragraph** about a person includes these ideas:

- An introductory sentence that gets the reader's attention

- Some adjectives that help the reader picture or imagine how the person looks

- Details or examples that tell what the person does

Look at this word web. It describes how Rip Van Winkle looks and acts at the beginning of the story.

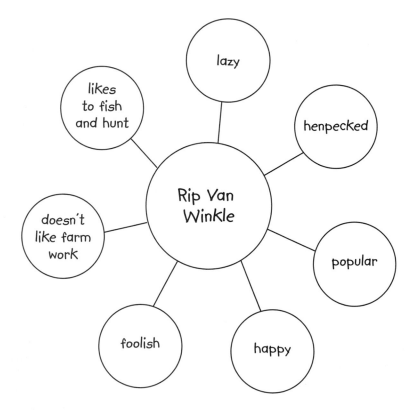

Write a description of someone you know or have read about. Think about the person you want to describe. What does he or she look like? What is special about the person? Make a word web to organize your ideas.

4

A Day's Wait

A story by Ernest Hemingway

About the Author

Ernest Hemingway was born in Oak Park, Illinois, in
1899. As a boy, he spent vacations in the woods of
Michigan, which became the setting for some of his
best-known stories. In World War I, Hemingway was a
Red Cross ambulance driver. Three of his best novels—
The Sun Also Rises, A Farewell to Arms, and *For Whom
the Bell Tolls*—take place in Europe during or after a
war. Indeed, war is central to most of Hemingway's
writing. What is important to him is the way the
characters behave in battle and how they face the
difficulties of life. Hemingway's short stories have
influenced generations of American writers. Much of
the meaning in his stories lies under the surface of his
clean, clear writing style. After publishing his famous
short novel *The Old Man and the Sea* in 1952,
Hemingway was awarded the Pulitzer Prize and the
Nobel Prize for literature. Hemingway died in 1961 by
ending his own life.

Before You Read

About "A Day's Wait"

Characters
Schatz, a nine-year-old boy; Schatz's father, the narrator; the doctor

Plot
A boy called Schatz is sick with influenza. His father reassures him that he will be fine. But Schatz cannot stop worrying. In time Schatz's father finds out why his son is so worried.

Setting
Time: 1920s
Place: the boy's bedroom

Theme
A little knowledge can sometimes do more harm than good.

Build Background

Epidemics

As you may know, the illness influenza is called "the flu." It is very contagious. One person can easily catch the flu from another person. When many people in one area catch the flu, it is called an epidemic. In the story you will read, there is a "light epidemic."

Flu epidemics can be very serious. A worldwide epidemic in 1918 killed between 20 million and 40 million people. Today, modern medicine helps control flu epidemics.

Think back to a time when you were home in bed with an illness. What did you think about? Were you worried? Sad? Bored? Describe your feelings about being ill.

Key Words

Read these sentences. Try to understand each word in boldfaced type by looking at the other words in the sentence. Use a dictionary to check your ideas. Write each word and its meaning in your notebook.

epidemic

fever

influenza

pneumonia

Schatz

1. An **epidemic** of the flu means that many people in one area have the illness.

2. The boy's temperature was high, and a high **fever** is one symptom of the flu.

3. "The flu" is a short name for the illness known as **influenza.**

4. When the boy had **pneumonia,** his lungs filled with liquid, making it hard for him to breathe.

5. The man called his son **Schatz,** which is a German word that means "treasure."

Reading Strategy

Monitor Your Comprehension

Monitor, or check, **your comprehension** as you read. For example, ask yourself, "Did I understand that paragraph? What didn't I understand?" If you find a part of a story that you don't understand, follow these steps:

- Reread that part of the story.

- Try to retell the story in your own words.

- List ideas from the story that are hard to understand.

- Write questions about things that you don't understand.

- Look for answers to your questions in the story, or discuss them with your teacher.

A Day's Wait

A story by Ernest Hemingway

He came into the room to shut the windows while we were still in bed and I saw he looked ill. He was shivering, his face was white, and he walked slowly as though it ached to move.

"What's the matter, Schatz?"

"I've got a headache."

"You better go back to bed."

"No. I'm all right."

"You go to bed. I'll see you when I'm dressed."

But when I came downstairs he was dressed, sitting by the fire, looking a very sick and miserable boy of nine years. When I put my hand on his forehead I knew he had a fever.

"You go up to bed," I said, "you're sick."

"I'm all right," he said.

When the doctor came he took the boy's temperature.

"What is it?" I asked him.

"One hundred and two."

Downstairs, the doctor left three different medicines in different colored capsules with instructions for giving them. One was to bring down the fever, another a purgative,[1] the third to overcome an acid condition. The germs of influenza can only exist in an acid condition, he explained. He seemed to know all about influenza and said there was nothing to worry about if the fever did not go above one hundred and four degrees. This was a light epidemic of flu and there was no danger if you avoided pneumonia.

Back in the room I wrote the boy's temperature down and made a note of the time to give the various capsules.

"Do you want me to read to you?"

---

[1]*purgative:* a medicine that cleans out the body

70

"All right. If you want to," said the boy. His face was very white and there were dark areas under his eyes. He lay still in the bed and seemed very detached from what was going on.

I read aloud from Howard Pyle's *Book of Pirates*; but I could see he was not following what I was reading.

"How do you feel, Schatz?" I asked him.

"Just the same, so far," he said.

I sat at the foot of the bed and read to myself while I waited for it to be time to give another capsule. It would have been natural for him to go to sleep, but when I looked up he was looking at the foot of the bed, looking very strangely.

"Why don't you try to sleep? I'll wake you up for the medicine."

"I'd rather stay awake."

After a while he said to me, "You don't have to stay in here with me, Papa, if it bothers you."

"It doesn't bother me."

"No, I mean you don't have to stay if it's going to bother you."

I thought perhaps he was a little lightheaded, and after giving him the prescribed capsules at eleven o'clock I went out for a while.

It was a bright, cold day, the ground covered with a sleet that had frozen so that it seemed as if all the bare trees, the bushes, the cut brush and all the grass and the bare ground had been varnished with ice. I took the young Irish setter for a little walk up the road and along a frozen creek, but it was difficult to stand or walk on the glassy surface and the red dog slipped and slithered and I fell twice, hard, once dropping my gun and having it slide away over the ice.

We flushed a covey of quail[2] under a high clay bank with overhanging brush and I killed two as they went out of sight over the top of the bank. Some of the covey lit[3] in trees, but most of them scattered into brush piles and it was necessary to jump on the ice-coated mounds of brush several times before they would flush. Coming out while you were poised unsteadily on the icy, springy brush they made difficult shooting and I killed two, missed five, and started back pleased to have found a covey close to the house and happy there were so many left to find another day.

At the house, they said the boy had refused to let anyone come into the room.

"You can't come in," he said. "You mustn't get what I have."

I went up to him and found him in exactly the position I had left him, white-faced, but with the tops of his cheeks flushed by the fever, staring still, as he had stared, at the foot of the bed.

I took his temperature.

"What is it?"

"Something like a hundred," I said. It was one hundred and two and four tenths.

[2]*covey:* small group of birds
[3]*lit:* in this context, the word means "came down and settled"

"It was a hundred and two," he said.

"Who said so?"

"The doctor."

"Your temperature is all right," I said. "It's nothing to worry about."

"I don't worry," he said, "but I can't keep from thinking."

"Don't think," I said. "Just take it easy."

"I'm taking it easy," he said and looked straight ahead. He was evidently holding tight onto himself about something.

"Take this with water."

"Do you think it will do any good?"

"Of course it will."

I sat down and opened the *Pirate* book and commenced to read, but I could see he was not following, so I stopped.

"About what time do you think I'm going to die?" he asked.

"What?"

"About how long will it be before I die?"

"You aren't going to die. What's the matter with you?"

"Oh, yes, I am. I heard him say a hundred and two."

"People don't die with a fever of one hundred and two. That's a silly way to talk."

"I know they do. At school in France, the boys told me you can't live with forty-four degrees. I've got a hundred and two."

He had been waiting to die all day, ever since nine o'clock in the morning.

"You poor Schatz," I said. "It's like miles and kilometers. You know, like how many kilometers we make when we do seventy miles in the car?"

"Oh," he said.

But his gaze at the foot of the bed relaxed slowly. The hold over himself relaxed too, finally, and the next day it was very slack[4] and he cried very easily at little things that were of no importance. ⌒

[4]*slack:* without energy; weak; soft

After You Read

Understand the Story

Answer these questions in your notebook. Write complete sentences.

1. Why did the father think that the boy was sick?
he is shivering

2. What was the boy's temperature?
202

3. Downstairs, when the boy was not listening, what did the doctor say to the father about the boy's temperature?
It's going to be fine

4. How did he behave while his father was reading to him?
not listen

5. What did the boy think was going to happen to him?
die

6. When the father explained about kilometers and miles, what did the boy understand? *afte about the C° and F°*

Elements of Literature

Theme

Read this passage from the story. Then answer the question.

> I sat down and opened the *Pirate* book and commenced to read, but I could see he was not following, so I stopped.
>
> . . . "About how long will it be before I die?"
>
> "You aren't going to die. What's the matter with you?"
>
> "Oh, yes, I am. I heard him say a hundred and two."
>
> "People don't die with a fever of one hundred and two. That's a silly way to talk."
>
> "I know they do. At school in France, the boys told me you can't live with forty-four degrees. I've got a hundred and two."

The theme of this story is that a little knowledge can sometimes do more harm than good. How does the passage above support this theme?

74

Discussion

Discuss in pairs or small groups.

1. The boy in Ernest Hemingway's story is nine years old. Do you think his behavior showed courage or fear? What words would you use to describe his character?

2. What words would you use to describe the father's character?

3. Did you enjoy reading this story? Why or why not?

Vocabulary

Choose the correct word. Write the completed sentences in your notebook.

1. The germs of _____ can only exist in an acid condition.
   a. Schatz **b.** influenza **c.** epidemic

2. An _____ of the flu means that many people in one area have the illness.
   a. importance **b.** influenza **c.** epidemic

3. The doctor said there was no danger if the boy avoided _____.
   a. covey **b.** pneumonia **c.** purgative

4. "How do you feel, _____?" the father asked the boy.
   a. Papa **b.** Pirate **c.** Schatz

5. A _____ of one hundred and two is not usually life-threatening.
   a. fever **b.** kilometer **c.** pneumonia

Word Study

Write the sentences below in your notebook. Complete each sentence with the correct form of the word. Use the chart to help you. The first one has been done for you.

Noun	Verb	Adjective
relaxation	relax	relaxing, relaxed
commencement	commence	commencing
prescription	prescribe	prescribing, prescribed
detachment	detach	detached
poise	poise	poised

1. There was no sign of _____relaxation_____ in the way the boy kept
   relaxation/relaxed

   a tight hold on himself throughout the day.

2. At the _____ of his illness, the boy claimed
   commencement /commence

   to be "all right" and didn't want to go back to bed.

3. The doctor needed to _____ various colored
   prescribe /prescribing

   capsules.

4. The father noticed, but did not understand, the boy's

   _____ from what was going on around him.
   detachment/detach

5. At one moment during the hunt, the Irish setter was stiffly

   _____ like an arrow, pointing his nose at the quail.
   poise/poised

76

Extension Activity

Fahrenheit or Celsius

The young boy in "A Day's Wait" confused the two measures of temperature, Fahrenheit and Celsius (also called Centigrade). As you have read, this confusion led him to worry needlessly.

A. Read about Fahrenheit and Celsius.

Temperature is a measure of heat. It is expressed in units called degrees. The symbol ° stands for degrees. Fahrenheit is a measure of temperature that is used in the United States. Most other countries in the world use the Celsius scale. Look at this chart about the two measures of temperature.

	Fahrenheit	Celsius
Water freezes	32°	0°
Water boils	212°	100°
Average body temperature	98.6°	37°

B. Copy each statement about temperature in your notebook. Write *true* if the statement is true, or *false* if the statement is false. Use the chart above to help you.

1. You are probably sick if you have a temperature of 101° Fahrenheit.

2. It can snow if the temperature is 65° Fahrenheit.

3. You wear a winter coat to go outside if the temperature is 20° Fahrenheit.

4. If your temperature is 37° Celsius, you do not have a fever.

5. You can boil an egg in water that is 50° Celsius.

6. The temperature of 32° Fahrenheit is the same as 0° Celsius.

Writing Practice

Write a Summary

A **summary** is a short review of the important information in a story. When you write a summary, you retell the most important ideas.

Read this summary of the first part of "A Day's Wait."

> A nine-year-old boy was sick with the flu. The doctor told his father that he had a temperature of 102 degrees. The doctor left medicine for the boy. He told his father that the boy would be all right if his temperature did not go over 104 degrees. The boy seemed very upset. He told the father not to stay.

Read each of the questions that follow. Continue the summary of "A Day's Wait" by writing answers to the questions.

1. While the father was away, what did the boy refuse to do?

2. Did he think his temperature was 102° Fahrenheit or 102° Celsius?

3. What had he been waiting all day for?

4. What did his father explain to him?

5. Did the boy understand his mistake, or not?

6. How did the boy behave the next day?

A Day's Wait

A Mystery of Heroism

Adapted from the story by Stephen Crane

About the Author

Stephen Crane was born in 1871 in Newark, New Jersey. After some schooling at Lafayette College and Syracuse University, he became a journalist in New York City, writing for different newspapers. His experiences in New York led to his first novel, *Maggie: A Girl of the Streets,* which he completed when he was only twenty. This book was a work of social realism that was very unusual for its time. In 1895, still only twenty-four, Crane published *The Red Badge of Courage,* a novel about a young soldier in the American Civil War. This book is still widely read today. In 1897, Crane traveled to England, where he became friends with the writers Joseph Conrad, Henry James, and H. G. Wells. Crane died of the disease tuberculosis in 1900. He was only twenty-nine, but his stories, novels, articles, and poetry filled twelve volumes when collected together in 1926.

Before You Read

About "A Mystery of Heroism"

Characters
Fred Collins, an infantry soldier; Fred's companions; a wounded artillery officer; the captain; another officer

Plot
Fred Collins is an infantry soldier. He and his company are caught in heavy fighting in a meadow. Collins decides that he will go to get water. He is not afraid and wonders if he is a hero. He manages to get the water, but on his way back from the well, his courage is tested again.

Setting
Time: 1861–1865, a time during the Civil War
Place: a battlefield somewhere in the South

Theme
A heroic act is something that is courageous and noble. Even the smallest act can be heroic.

Build Background

American Civil War

This story takes place on a battlefield during the American Civil War (1861–1865). The southern states wanted to separate from the United States and form a new country of their own. The South wanted slavery, but the North did not. The northern army wore blue uniforms. The southern army wore gray uniforms. Hundreds of thousands of young men lost their lives. The North won the war, the United States remained as one country, and enslaved people were freed.

What do you know about the American Civil War? Share what you know with a partner.

Key Words

Read these sentences. Try to understand each word in boldfaced type by looking at the other words in the sentence. Use a dictionary to check your ideas. Write each word and its meaning in your notebook.

1. The **artillery** was the unit of men responsible for firing the weapons on the field.

2. The soldiers had **canteens,** metal containers filled with water.

3. Each regiment was divided into smaller groups called **companies.**

4. They waited for the **infantry,** the soldiers who fought on foot.

5. The fighting men on a hill saw the others below them in a **meadow,** or small field.

6. The two companies of fighting men made up the **regiment.**

7. The **shells** were like little bombs exploding all over the fields.

artillery

canteens

companies

infantry

meadow

regiment

shells

Reading Strategy

Visualize

Visualizing means imagining, or picturing, something in your mind. Authors want readers to visualize, or see, the characters, events, and places in a story. An author's descriptive words help readers visualize. Descriptive words can be adjectives, verbs, or nouns.

> The **dark blue uniforms** of the men were **coated** with **dust** from the **endless struggle** between the **two armies.**

Adjectives: *dark, blue, coated, endless, two*

Nouns: *uniforms, dust, struggle, armies*

As you read, try to visualize the characters, places, and events of the story.

A Mystery of Heroism

Adapted from the story by Stephen Crane

The dark blue uniforms of the men were coated with dust from the endless struggle between the two armies. They were so dirty that the regiment almost seemed part of the clay bank which shielded the soldiers from the exploding shells. On the top of the hill, the big guns were arguing in enormous roars with the enemy's guns across from them. To the eyes of the infantry soldiers below, the artillerymen, the guns, the horses, the waiting shells, were distinctly arranged against the blue sky. When a gun was fired, a huge red flash like lightning appeared low in the heavens. The artillerymen wore white trousers, which somehow emphasized their legs, and when they ran and crowded in little groups following orders from the shouting officers, they impressed the men of the infantry.

Fred Collins of A Company infantry was saying: "Thunder,[1] I wish I had a drink. Isn't there any water around here?" Then someone yelled, "There goes the flag!"

As the eyes of half the regiment swept across the field in one machine-like movement, they caught the picture of a horse in a violent leap of a death. Its rider leaned back with a bent arm and fingers spread before his face. On the ground was the bright red terror of an exploding shell shooting flashes of flame. The torn flag swung clear of the rider's back as both horse and man fell forward heavily onto the ground. In the air was a smell like an enormous blazing fire.

Sometimes the infantry soldiers looked down at the fair little meadow which spread at their feet. Its long, green grass was rolling gently in the light wind. Beyond it was the gray form of a farmhouse half torn to pieces by shells and by the busy axes of soldiers who had used the wood for their fires. The line of an old fence was now marked by long weeds and by an occasional wooden post. A shell

---

[1]*thunder:* here, the word is used as a strong exclamation, like a curse, but without particular meaning

had blown the well-house to fragments. Little lines of smoke rose upward from the hot ashes of the place where the barn had stood.

From beyond a curtain of green woods there came the sound of some huge struggle, as if two animals the size of islands were fighting. At a distance, there were occasional appearances of swift-moving men, horses, gun-wagons, flags. Along with the sharp crashing of infantry shots, the wild shouting and curses and cheers of men could be heard.

The big guns on the hill now engaged in a frightful exchange with the enemy's artillery. The white legs of the gunners hurried this way and that way and the officers redoubled their shouts. One of the men was suddenly hit and thrown to the ground, and his maddened companions dragged away his torn body in their struggle to escape from the confusion and danger. A young soldier on horseback cursed and shouted in his saddle[2] and jerked at the straps in his hands. An officer shouted an order so violently that his voice broke and ended the sentence in a high scream.

The company of the infantry that was most open to danger began to move slowly toward greater protection near the hill. There was the clank of steel against steel.

An artillery officer rode down from the guns and passed them, holding his right arm in his left hand. And it was as if this arm was not at all a part of him, but belonged to another man. His large quiet horse moved slowly. The officer's face was grimed with dirt and wet with sweat, and his uniform was so wrinkled that it seemed he had been in a direct fight with an enemy. He smiled bitterly when the men stared at him. He turned his horse toward the meadow.

Collins of A Company said again: "I wish I had a drink. I bet there's water in that old well over there!"

"Yes; but how're you going to get it?"

The little meadow that lay between the soldiers and the well was now suffering a terrible attack of shells. Its green and beautiful calm had vanished completely. Brown earth was being thrown up in monstrous handfuls. The tall young grass was being murdered—

---

[2] *saddle:* leather seat for a rider on a horse

84

torn, burned, cut to pieces. Some curious fortune of the battle had made this gentle little meadow the object of the red hate of the shells, and each one as it exploded seemed like a horrible curse in the face of an innocent girl.

The wounded officer who was riding across this expanse said to himself, "Why, they couldn't shoot any harder if the whole army was gathered here!"

A shell struck the gray ruins of the house, and, after the explosion, the shattered wall fell in fragments, with the sound of thunder crashing sharply in a sea-storm. Indeed, the infantry, pausing in the shelter of the bank, looked like men standing upon a shore staring at the madness of a wild winter ocean. The angel of disaster had turned its glance on the big guns upon the hill. Fewer white-legged men labored around them. A shell had hit one of the gun-wagons, and after the flash and smoke and dust and anger of the blow were gone, it was possible to see white legs stretched horizontally upon the ground.

In a space to the rear of the guns stood the artillery horses with their noses pointing at the fight. Their business was to drag the gun-wagons out of the destruction, or into it, or wherever else those strange humans demanded. Their hearts might beat wildly, but they could not forget the iron laws of man's control over them. In this line of speechless observers there had been unending and terrible destruction. From the mess of bleeding horses on the ground, the men could see one animal raising its wounded body with its forelegs and turning its nose with silent, astonishing grace toward the sky.

Some of his companions joked with Collins about his thirst. "Well, if you want a drink so bad, why don't you go get it?"

"Well, I will in a minute if you don't shut up."

A private in B Company, to the rear, looked out over the meadow and then turned to a companion and said, "Look there, Jim." It was the wounded officer from the infantry who had started to ride across the meadow, supporting his right arm carefully with his left hand. This man had met with a shell, apparently at a time when no one observed him. He could be seen lying face downward with one foot stretched across the body of his dead horse. One of the horse's legs extended upward precisely as stiff as an iron post. Around this motionless pair the shells still roared and howled.

There was a quarrel in A Company. Collins was shaking his fist in the face of some laughing companions. "Curse you! I'm not afraid to go! If you say much, I *will* go!"

"Of course you will! You'll run right through that there meadow, won't you?"

Collins said in a terrible voice: "You just watch me, now!" At this dark warning, his companions broke into renewed laughter and cheers.

Collins gave them a dark look and went to find his captain. The captain was talking with another officer of the regiment.

"Captain," said Collins, standing stiffly at attention, "Captain, I want to get permission to go get some water from that well over there."

The captain and the other officer swung around at the same moment and stared across the meadow. The captain laughed. "You must be pretty thirsty, Collins!"

"Yes, sir; I am."

"Well—ah," said the captain. After a moment he asked: "Can't you wait?"

"No, sir."

The other officer was watching Collins's face. "Look here, my boy," he said in a serious sort of voice. "Look here, my boy." Collins was not a boy. "Don't you think that's taking big risks for a little drink of water?"

"I don't know," said Collins uncomfortably. Some of the anger at his companions, which perhaps had forced him into this affair, was beginning to vanish. "I don't know whether it is or not."

The captain and the other officer observed him for a while.

"Well," said the captain finally.

"Well," said the other officer, "If you want to go, then go."

Collins stood more stiffly still. "Thank you, sir!"

As he moved away the captain called after him, "Take some of the other boys' canteens with you and hurry back now."

"Yes, sir, I will."

The two officers looked at each other then, for it had suddenly occurred to them that they didn't know whether Collins wanted to go or not.

They turned to look at Collins and as they observed him surrounded by his eagerly talking companions, the captain said, "Well, by thunder! I guess he's going."

Collins seemed like a man dreaming. In the middle of all the questions, the advice, the warnings, all the excited talk of the men, he maintained a curious silence.

They were very busy preparing him for his attempt. When they inspected him carefully, it was somewhat as if they were examining a horse before a race, and they were amazed and puzzled by the whole affair. Their astonishment was expressed in strange repetitions.

"Are you sure you're going?" they demanded again and again.

"Certainly I am," cried Collins at last, furiously.

He walked angrily away from them. He was swinging five or six canteens from their straps. It seemed that his hat would not remain firmly on his head, and he often reached and pulled it down over his forehead.

There was a general movement in the line of soldiers. The long animal-like thing moved slightly. Its four hundred eyes were turned upon the figure of Collins.

"Well, sir, if that isn't the darnedest thing. I never thought Fred Collins had the blood in him for that kind of business."

"What's he going to do, anyhow?"

"He's going to that well there after water."

"We aren't dying of thirst, are we? That's foolishness."

"Well, somebody gave him the idea and he's doing it."

"Well, he must be a desperate man."

When Collins faced the meadow and walked away from the regiment he was half conscious that a divide, a deep valley of pride, was suddenly between him and his companions. He had blindly been led by curious emotions and had taken on a responsibility to walk squarely up to the face of death.

But he was not sure that he wished to take back his intention even if he could do so without shame. As a matter of truth, he was sure of very little. He was mainly surprised.

In addition, he wondered why he did not feel some sharp pain of fear cutting his sense like a knife. He wondered at this because human expression had said loudly for centuries that men should feel afraid of certain things and that all men who did not feel this fear were very special, were heroes.

He was then a hero. He suffered that disappointment which we would all have if we discovered that we were ourselves capable of those brave acts which we most admire in history and legend. This, then, was a hero. In the end, heroes were not much.

No, it could not be true. He could not be a hero. Heroes had no shame in their lives. As for him, he remembered borrowing eighty dollars from a friend and promising to pay it back the next day, and then avoiding that friend for ten months. When at home his mother had awakened him for the early work of his life on the farm, he had often been easy to anger, moody, childish, devilish, and his mother had died since he had come to the war.

He saw that in this matter of the well, the canteens, the shells, he was almost like a thief in the land of brave acts.

He was now about thirty steps from his companions. The regiment had just turned its many faces toward him. Before him was the chaos of the fight.

Collins suddenly felt that two devil's fingers were pressed into his ears. He could see nothing but red arrows of flame. He almost fell from the force of this explosion, but he made a mad rush for the house. He viewed it as a man up to the neck in crashing waves might view the shore. In the air, little pieces of shell howled, and the

earthquake explosions drove him mad with their monstrous roar. As he ran the canteens knocked together with a rhythmical tinkling.

As he neared the house each detail of the scene became precise and clear. He was aware of some bricks of the vanished chimney lying on the ground. There was a door hanging strangely from its frame.

Bullets from the distant woods mixed with the shells and the pieces of shells until the air was torn in all directions by whistles, screams, howls. When he came to the well, he threw himself face downward and looked deep into its darkness. There were hidden points of silver shining some feet from the surface. He took one of the canteens and, unfastening its top, swung it down by the strap. The water flowed slowly in with a lazy gurgle.

And now as he lay with his face turned away he was suddenly struck with the terror. It came upon his heart and surrounded it like iron fingers. All the power faded from his muscles. For a moment, he was no more than a dead man.

The canteen filled with a maddening slowness in the manner of all bottles. Soon he recovered his strength and directed a screaming curse at it. He leaned over until it seemed as if he intended to push water into it with his hands. He stared down into the well with eyes that shone like pieces of metal.

There was the nearby thunder of a shell. Red light shone through the boiling smoke and made a pink reflection on part of the wall of the well. Collins pulled out his arm and canteen as if from a hot fire. He stood up suddenly and stared and hesitated. On the ground near him lay the old bucket with a length of rusty chain. He lowered it swiftly into the well. The bucket struck the water and then, turning lazily over, sank. When he drew it out, hand reaching over shaking hand, it knocked often against the walls of the well and spilled some of its contents.

In running with a filled bucket, a man can use only one kind of form. So through this terrible field over which screamed the angels of death, Collins ran in the manner of a farmer chased out of the dairy by a bull.

His face went staring white with expectation—expectation of a blow that would throw him around and down. He would fall as he had seen other men fall, the life knocked out of them so suddenly that their knees and heads hit the ground together. He saw the long blue line of the regiment, but his companions were standing looking at him from the edge of an impossible star. He was aware of some deep wheel markings and the footprints of animals in the dirt beneath his feet.

The artillery officer who had fallen in this meadow had been making groans in the teeth of the storm of sound. These cries, drawn from him by his suffering, were heard only by shells and bullets. When wild-eyed Collins came running, this officer raised himself. His face wrinkled and whitened from pain, he was about to release some great begging cry. But suddenly his face straightened and he called: "Say, young man, give me a drink of water, will you?"

Collins had no room in his emotions for surprise. He was mad from the threats of destruction.

"I can't," he screamed, and in this reply was a full description of his shaking expectation. His hat was gone, his hair stood up on end. His clothes made it appear that he had been dragged over the ground by his heels. He ran on.

The officer's head sank down and one elbow bent. His foot was still stretched over the body of his horse and the other leg was under it.

But Collins turned. He came running back. His face had now turned gray and in his eyes was all terror. "Here it is! Here it is!"

The officer was like a man weakened by too much drink. His arm bent like a thin branch. His head fell forward as if his neck was soft wood. He was sinking to the ground, to lie face downward.

Collins grabbed him by the shoulder. "Here it is. Here's your drink. Turn over! Turn over, man, for goodness sake!"

With Collins pulling at his shoulder, the officer turned his body and fell with his face turned toward that region where the unspeakable noises of the shells lived. There was the faintest shadow of a smile on his lips as he looked at Collins. He gave a sigh, a little primitive breath like that from a child.

Collins tried to hold the bucket steadily, but his shaking hands caused the water to splash all over the face of the dying man. Then he grabbed it away and ran on.

The regiment gave him a welcoming roar. The grimed faces were wrinkled in laughter.

His captain waved the bucket away. "Give it to the men!"

Two cheerful minor officers were the first to gain possession of it. They played over it in their fashion.

When one tried to drink, the other playfully knocked his elbow. "Don't, Billie! You'll make me spill it," said the one. The other laughed.

Suddenly there was a curse, the thud of wood on the ground, and a swift murmur of astonishment from the soldiers. The two officers stared angrily at each other. The bucket lay on the ground empty. ✎

After You Read

Understand the Story

Answer these questions in your notebook. Write complete sentences.

1. What armies were fighting the battle in this story?

2. What did Fred Collins want?

3. What did the captain and another officer give Collins permission to do?

4. Where did Collins go to get water, and what did he finally put the water in?

5. Who did Collins meet on his way back to his company?

6. What happened to the water that Collins had risked his life to get?

Elements of Literature

Similes

A **simile** is a comparison between two things using the word *like*. Similes usually compare two things that are not alike. Read these examples from the story.

- Collins wondered why he did not feel some sharp pain of *fear* cutting his sense *like a knife.*

- The *terror* came upon his heart and surrounded it *like iron fingers.*

- He stared down into the well with *eyes* that shone *like pieces of metal.*

In each example, the words in italics tell you which things are being compared. In the first example, fear is compared to a knife. In the second example, terror is compared to iron fingers. What two things are being compared in the third example?

How do similes help you visualize what you read?

Discussion

Discuss in pairs or small groups.

The title of Stephen Crane's story is "A Mystery of Heroism." Where is the mystery in Collins's act? Choose one of these answers, or think of a different answer. Explain your choice.

a. The mystery is whether Collins's act was heroic or not.

b. The mystery is what made Collins act as he did.

c. The mystery is why acts of courage seem meaningless in a war.

Vocabulary

Choose the correct word. Write the completed sentences in your notebook.

1. The artillerymen impressed the men of the _____.
   a. infantry   **b.** shells   **c.** canteens

2. The bank shielded the soldiers from the exploding _____.
   a. infantry   **b.** shells   **c.** meadow

3. The captain was talking with another officer of the _____.
   a. regiment   **b.** shells   **c.** bullets

4. Fred Collins was a soldier in the A _____.
   a. Meadow   **b.** Canteen   **c.** Company

5. Collins filled one of the _____ with water.
   a. artillery   **b.** canteens   **c.** companies

6. The big guns on the hill engaged in a frightful exchange with the enemy's _____.
   a. artillery   **b.** canteen   **c.** meadow

7. The green grass of the _____ was rolling in the wind.
   a. regiment   **b.** artillery   **c.** meadow

Word Study

Write the sentences below in your notebook. Complete each sentence with the correct form of the word. Use the chart to help you. The first one has been done for you.

Noun	Adjective	Adverb
emphasis	emphatic	emphatically
destruction	destructive	destructively
impression	impressive	impressively
observation	observant	observantly
astonishment	astonished, astonishing	astonishingly
despair, desperation	desperate	desperately

1. "I'm not afraid to go!" Collins declared ___*emphatically*___.
   emphasis/emphatically

2. Shells caused the _____ of the farmhouse.
   destruction/destructive

3. The uniforms, actions, and shouts of the artillerymen were _____ to the men of the infantry.
   impressive/impressively

4. Only the most _____ soldiers noticed that the
   observation/observant
   wounded officer had turned his horse toward the meadow.

5. The men were _____ to see Collins turn back to
   astonishment/astonished
   give water to the wounded officer.

6. The artillery soldiers _____ dragged their
   despair/desperately
   companion away from the shells exploding in front of them.

Extension Activity

Civil War Literature

"A Mystery of Heroism" is set during the American Civil War. Stephen Crane, the author, also wrote a novel set during the Civil War. It is called *The Red Badge of Courage*.

A. Read about *The Red Bad of Courage*.

> *The Red Badge of Courage* was first published in 1895. In the novel, Stephen Crane painted a clear and haunting picture of war. The story is told from the point of view of a young soldier, Henry Fleming. He is in the Union Army, the army of the North. Henry prepares for his first battle, and then his second, and confronts all his different feelings.

B. Make a list of titles of books, short stories, and movies that are set during the Civil War.

- Work with a small group.
- Research the names of other short stories, books, or movie titles that are about the Civil War. Use the websites of booksellers or other Internet sources. Or use your school library.
- Write each story or book title and its author.
- Write each movie title.
- Make a three-column chart on poster paper.
- List titles under these headings: *Books*, *Stories*, and *Movies*.
- Display the chart in the classroom.

Writing Practice

Write an Expository Paragraph

Expository writing explains something. Expository writing gives factual information about a subject. A writer includes details and examples to explain the information.

Here are some things to remember when writing an expository paragraph:

- Make sure that your paragraph has one main idea about the topic. The main idea should be stated in the topic sentence.

- Use facts to support your main idea.

- Make your explanations simple and clear.

Read this expository paragraph about one of the most famous battles of the Civil War.

> The Battle of Gettysburg was an important battle of the American Civil War. The battle was fought in July 1863. General Robert E. Lee led the southern army, called the Confederate Army. General George Gordon Meade led the northern army, called the Union Army. After a bitter fight, with many lives lost, General Lee's army lost and was pushed back. Many people believe that the Battle of Gettysburg led to the victory of the Northern army.

Think of a subject that you know about, or want to learn about. Look up information about the subject on the Internet or in an encyclopedia. Write an expository paragraph that gives information about the topic.

Hope Deferred

Adapted from the story by Alice Dunbar-Nelson

About the Author

Alice Dunbar-Nelson was born in New Orleans, Louisiana, in 1875. She began teaching as soon as she graduated from college. She published her first book of short stories and poems, *Violets and Other Tales,* in 1897. Around that time Dunbar-Nelson moved to Brooklyn, New York. She began to exchange letters with the poet Paul Laurence Dunbar, and they were married in 1898. The marriage did not last. After separating from Dunbar in 1902, Dunbar-Nelson moved to Wilmington, Delaware. There she worked as a teacher and school administrator. In 1916, she married Robert J. Nelson, a journalist, politician, and civil rights activist. Dunbar-Nelson herself worked passionately to protect the civil rights of African Americans and women. For the rest of her life she remained active as a journalist, activist, public speaker, and writer. Dunbar-Nelson died in 1935.

Before You Read

About "Hope Deferred"

Characters
Louis Edwards, a trained civil engineer; Margaret Edwards, his wife; Hanan, the chief clerk at the Monarch Company; Adams, a restaurant owner

Plot
Louis Edwards is a trained civil engineer, but because he is African American, no one will hire him. He and his wife need money desperately, but Edwards refuses to give up hope. Finally, he takes a job as a waiter. All goes well until one awful night.

Setting
Time: early 1900s, August
Place: a city, somewhere between the North and the South

Theme
It can seem impossible to make a dream come true, but a strong person keeps trying.

Build Background

Civil Rights
In the story you will read, Louis Edwards comes face to face with discrimination. Discrimination is the unfair treatment of another person based on race, religion, gender, or country of birth. In Edwards's case, the issue is race—he is African American. In 1964, President Lyndon Baines Johnson asked Congress to pass a Civil Rights Act. This law made racial discrimination illegal. It also forced employers to offer equal employment opportunities to members of every race.

Do you know other stories, books, or movies about the issue of discrimination? If so, talk about them with your classmates.

Key Words

Read these sentences. Try to understand each word in boldfaced type by looking at the other words in the sentence. Use a dictionary to check your ideas. Write each word and its meaning in your notebook.

civil
   engineer
contempt
Negroes
poverty
strike

1. Louis Edwards was a **civil engineer.** He was trained to build bridges and roads.

2. The man at the company spoke with **contempt,** as if he hated Louis.

3. **Negroes** is a name used to describe people of African heritage.

4. Louis and Margaret knew **poverty.** They had very little money for food, shelter, and clothing.

5. The men were on **strike.** They refused to work until they received better pay.

Reading Strategy

Predict

As you read a story, you can **predict,** or guess, what will happen next. Follow these steps as you read:

- Stop reading from time to time and ask yourself, "What will happen next?"

- Look for clues in the story and the pictures.

- Think about what you already know about how people usually act.

- Think about your own experiences.

Continue reading to see if your prediction is correct.

Hope Deferred

Adapted from the story by Alice Dunbar-Nelson

The direct rays of the August sun beat down on the city. Women on the sidewalks wore light clothes that showed a maximum of form and a minimum of good taste. Fat men wiped the sweat from their red faces, entered bars for a cooling drink, and came out redder and sweatier. The presence of small, dark-skinned, poorly clothed boys told that the city, if not really southern, was at least on the borderland between North and South.

Edwards joined the sweating crowd in the hot, humid air and wiped his face with the rest. His shoes were dusty, his shirt wilted. As he saw himself in the mirror of a shop window, he smiled grimly. "Hardly a man to present himself before one of the Lords of Creation to ask a favor," he told himself.

Edwards was young, so young that he had not outgrown his ideals. Instead of allowing that to happen, he had chosen someone to share them with him. And he knew that a woman who is willing to face poverty for her husband's ideals is a treasure far above diamonds. But ideals do not always satisfy the needs of the body for food, shelter, and clothing. And it was those needs that pushed Edwards—tired, wilted, and discouraged—out into the August sunshine.

The elevator boy directed him to an office where a man looked up impatiently from his desk. The windows of the room opened onto a yard where green treetops waved in a light, humid wind. An electric fan provided some coolness. And cool-looking leather chairs invited the dusty traveler to rest.

Edwards was not invited to rest, however. Cold gray eyes in a pale, bitter face stared at him with something like contempt. The voice was cold, icy, cutting.

"Sorry, Mr.—Er—but I won't be able to grant your job request."

His "Good-bye" in response to Edwards's reply was short and cold. It gave the impression of relief at the completion of an unpleasant job.

"Now where?" He had tried everything, and now the last door of hope in his mind closed. He walked slowly down the little side street that led home, drawn to it as a child in trouble is drawn to its mother.

Margaret met him at the door. Their faces lighted up with the glow that always shone there in each other's presence. She drew him into the green shade of the little room. Her eyes asked, though she didn't speak the question.

"No hope," he said. She sat down suddenly like one grown weak. "If only I could just hold out, little one," he said. "But we need food, clothes—and only money buys them, you know."

"Perhaps it would have been better if we hadn't married," she suggested. That thought had been in her mind often lately.

"Because you are tired of poverty?" he asked, though the smile on his lips answered the question.

She rose and put her arms around his neck. "You know better than that. But if you did not have me, you could live on less. You'd have a better chance to hold out until they could see your worth."

"I'm afraid they never will." He tried to keep his voice calm, but his words shook slightly. "The man I saw today was my last hope. He is the chief clerk at the Monarch Company. What he says controls the opinions of others. I wanted to talk to the company president, but he is a man who leaves details to those below him. And Mr. Hanan distrusted me from the first. I could feel his contempt. I could almost see it," he added bitterly.

"We can wait. Your chance will come," she said softly with a rare smile.

"But in the meantime . . ." he finished for her and paused himself.

A pile of bills was in the afternoon mail, telling him unnecessarily that he owed money and should pay it immediately. Those bills drove Edwards back out into the wilting sun. He knew the main street from end to end. He had walked so often in the past four months—at first happily, then hopefully, at last wearily—up and down its length.

The usual idle crowd stood in front of a large bulletin board where announcements and advertisements were pinned. Edwards joined the group automatically. "A meeting of my companions in poverty," he said to himself with an inner smile, and then listened idly to a voice at his side:

"We're becoming just like a big city, look at that!"

"That" was an item above the local team's baseball scores. Edwards looked at the bulletin, and the letters burned themselves like fire into his brain.

STRIKE SPREADS TO OUR CITY!

WAITERS AT ADAMS' RESTAURANT WALK OUT THIS MORNING!

"Good!" Edwards said aloud. And he turned and walked down the street with a lighter step than he had known for days.

The owner of Adams' restaurant looked neither like an Adams nor like a restaurant owner. He should have been somewhat red and somewhat fat and very American. Instead he was tall, wiry, and foreign looking. His front teeth stuck out over a full lower lip. His thin face was gray and his eyes were set far back in his head. They were the eyes of a man who looked very carefully and sharply at people.

"Of course I want waiters," he replied to Edwards's question. "Any fool knows that." He paused, drew his lower lip under his long teeth, and narrowed his eyes at Edwards. "But do I want colored waiters? Now, do I?"

"It seems to me there's no choice for you in the matter," said Edwards with good humor.

The reply seemed to amuse the restaurant owner greatly. He slapped the younger man on the back with a familiarity that was almost contemptuous.

"I guess I'll take you for head waiter." He seemed quite cheerful in spite of the disaster that the morning's strike had brought him. "Change into this white coat and go to work. Say, wait!" as Edwards began to move off, "What's your name?"

"Louis Edwards."

"Uh huh. Had any experience as a waiter?"

"Yes, some years ago, when I was at school."

"Uh huh. Then waiting isn't your general work?"

"No."

"Uh huh. What do you do for a living?

"I'm a civil engineer."

One eyebrow of the gray-faced Adams shot up, and he withdrew his lower lip entirely under his teeth. "Well, say man, if you're an engineer, why do you want to be strike-breaking here in a waiter's coat, eh?"

Edwards's face darkened, and he shrugged his shoulders. "They don't need me, I guess," he replied briefly. It was an effort, and the restaurant owner saw it, but his surprise was stronger than his sympathy.

"Don't need you with all that's going on at the Monarch works? Why, man, I'd have thought they would need every engineer in the state out there."

"I thought so, too. That's why I came here, but . . ."

"Say, kid, I'm sorry for you, I really am. You go on to work."

"And so," Edwards explained to Margaret after midnight, when he got home from his first day's work, "I became head waiter, first assistant, all the other waiters, chief boss, manager, and highest of the high, with all the advantages and glory of those positions."

Margaret was silent. She knew that no words of hers were needed then. They would only add to the heaviness in his heart. Nothing could be more bitter than this loss of his lifelong hopes, this lowering of his standards. She said nothing, but the pressure of her small brown hand in his meant more than words to both of them.

"It's so hard to be true to your ideals," he said.

If it was hard that night, it grew harder within the next few weeks. The waiters who were on strike were not at all happy about being replaced. They came to the restaurant every day, and they came with shouted threats and behavior that was ugly and dangerous. Through the restaurant's open door they threw rotten vegetables, mud, and stones. Adams shouted at them that he would run his own restaurant if he had to hire every African in America. The three or four men besides Edwards that he hired threatened every day to give up the battle. Edwards was the force that held them together. He used every argument, from the practical one of keeping a job now that they had one, to the idealistic one of keeping the place open for colored men for the future. He wiped the mud from his face, picked the rotten vegetables off the floor, and stood by Adams's side when the fight threatened to grow serious.

Adams seemed grateful. "Say, kid, I don't know what I'd have done without you. I mean it. Believe me, when you need a friend anywhere on Earth, just call on me, and I'll be there for you."

This was on the afternoon when the crowd in front of the restaurant included a number of men who had never worked there. That form of "sympathy" was all over town.

The humid August days melted into a hot September. The striking waiters slowly quieted down and annoyed Adams and his dark-skinned helpers less and less. Edwards did not complain about his situation. He felt, with the optimism of the idealist, that it was only for a little while. He had tried and failed to find work as an engineer for almost a year, but he was not defeated. He would explain carefully to Margaret, after a day's work, that it was only for a little while. He would earn enough money to allow them to get away. Then in some other place he would be able to stand taller, proud that his training had not been wasted.

He was reviewing these plans in his mind one Saturday night. It was at an hour when business in the restaurant was slow, and he leaned against the window looking at the crowd on the street. Saturday night in a small city, with the noise and excitement of cheap pleasures and fast action. Half-grown boys and girls, happy with their freedom on a humid Saturday night, crowded against each other, pushed in long lines, and boldly shouted insults they thought were funny. One crowd in particular attracted Edwards's attention. The girls were brave in short skirts and the smallest of blouses, the boys in loud red neckties and white trousers. They made a snake-line, boys and girls, hands on each other's shoulders, and danced through the crowd of shoppers, rudely bumping people left and right. Edwards lifted and eyebrow. "Now, if those were colored boys and girls . . ."

His thought was never finished, for a customer moved toward his table, and the critic of human life became once more the polite waiter.

He did not move a muscle of his face as he placed the glass of water on the table, handed the man a menu, and stood at attention waiting for the order. But he had recognized at first glance the half-contemptuous face of his old hope—Hanan, of the great Monarch Company that had no need for him. To Hanan, the man who brought his order was just one of the many servants who satisfied his daily needs and provided his pleasure when the cares of the day stopped pressing on his shoulders. He had not even looked at the man's face, and for this Edwards was grateful.

A new note had crept into the noise on the streets. There was in it now, not so much laughter and excitement as threat and anger. Edwards looked outside in some alarm as he returned to the table with Hanan's order. He knew this particular note in the noise of the streets, particularly on Saturday nights. It meant that the whole restaurant must be prepared for trouble. The snake-line had changed: Only the loud red neckties remained; the short skirts and small blouses had retreated to another corner. Something in the shouting attracted Hanan's attention, and he looked up wonderingly.

"What are they saying?" he asked. Edwards did not answer. He was so familiar with the old cry that he thought it unnecessary.

"Yah! Yah! Old Adams hires Negroes! Hires Negroes!"

"Why, that is so," Hanan looked up at Edwards' dark face for the first time. "This is something new at Adams's place. How did it happen?"

"We are strike-breakers," replied the waiter quietly, then he grew hot, for recognition came into Hanan's eyes.

"Oh, yes, I see. Aren't you the young man who asked me for a job as an engineer at the Monarch works?"

Edwards bowed. He could not answer. Hurt pride rose within him and made his eyes hot and his hands sweaty.

"Well,—er—I'm glad you've found a place to work. Very sensible of you, I'm sure. I should think, too, that it is work for which you are more qualified than engineering."

Edwards started to reply, but the hot words stopped at his lips. The shouting had reached a level that promised action. With the force of a ball shot from a large gun, a stone crashed through the glass of the long window. It hit Edwards's hand, bounced through the dishes on the tray he was delivering to the table, and spilled half its contents over Hanan's knee. He leapt to his feet angrily, trying to brush the remains of his dinner from his fine clothing. He turned angrily upon Edwards.

"That is criminally careless of you!" he shouted, his eyes glowing in his pale face. "You could have prevented that. You're not even a good waiter, much less an engineer!"

And then something exploded in the darker man's head. The long strain of the hopeless summer; the struggle of keeping together the men who worked under him in the restaurant; the heat, the sense of failure, and now this last injustice—all this entered his brain in a blinding flash. Reason, intelligence, all went into hiding except a main hatred, and a desire to push all his failure onto the man who, just now, represented the cause of it. He leapt at the white man's throat and threw him to the floor. They fought each other, struggling, biting like animals in the mess of food and dishes and overturned chairs.

The telephone rang insistently. Adams wiped his hands on a towel, and carefully moved a small paintbrush out of the way as he picked up the receiver.

"Hello!" he called. "Yes, this is Adams. Who? Uh huh. He wants to know if I'll help him get out of jail? Say, that kid's got softening of the brain. Of course not, let him serve his time. Making all that trouble in my place; why, I never saw such a thing! No, I don't ever want to see him again."

He hung up the receiver with a bang, and went back to painting his sign. He had almost finished, and he smiled at his work:

WAITERS WANTED. ONLY WHITE MEN NEED APPLY.

Out in the county workhouse, Edwards sat on his small bed, his head in his hands. He wondered what Margaret was doing all this long hot Sunday, if the tears were blinding her sight as they did his. Then he came to his feet as the jailor called his name. Margaret stood before him, her arms reaching toward him, her face shining with sympathy and tenderness.

"Margaret! You here, in this place?"

"Aren't you here?" she smiled bravely. "Did you think I wouldn't come to see you?"

"I can't believe I've brought you to this," he said. "Things couldn't be worse."

He told her the whole story. She quieted his fear and anger. Then she said, "How long will it be?"

"A long time, my dearest—and you?"

"I can go home and work," she answered quickly, "and wait for you, whether it's ten months or ten years—and then . . . ?"

"And then . . ." They stared into each other's eyes like frightened children. Suddenly he straightened up, and his face shone again with his strength of character.

"And then, my love," he said, "we will start all over again. Somewhere, I am needed. Somewhere in this world there is a need for dark-skinned men like me to dig and blast and build bridges and make straight the roads of the world. And I am going to find that place—with you."

She smiled back at him. "Only keep true to your ideals, Louis," she whispered, "and you will find the place. Your window faces south here, see? Look up and out of it all the time you are here. It is there, in our own southland, that we will realize our dream."

After You Read

Understand the Story

Answer these questions in your notebook. Write complete sentences.

1. What month is it when the story begins? What is the weather like? *Jan, dry*

2. Why couldn't Edwards get a job at the Monarch Company? *he don't have money*

3. Why did Adams give Edwards a job at the restaurant? *so he can earn money*

4. Why were people protesting outside Adams's Restaurant? *try to get work*

5. Why did Hanan blame Edwards for what happened the night when the rock came through the restaurant window? *Hanan did it*

6. What arguments did Edwards use to keep the other African American restaurant workers from giving up? *fighting*

Elements of Literature

Foreshadowing

Foreshadowing is using clues to suggest events that have not yet happened. Authors use foreshadowing to build tension or excitement. Read this passage from the story. Then answer the questions.

> Adams seemed grateful. "Say, kid, I don't know what I'd have done without you. I mean it. Believe me, when you need a friend anywhere on Earth, just call on me, and I'll be there for you."

How does the author use this paragraph to foreshadow later story events? What happens when Edwards does "call on" Adams for help?

Discussion

Discuss in pairs or small groups.

1. In your opinion, was Edwards right to attack Hanan in the restaurant? Why or why not? *No, you need to have a reason*

2. How do you think the author felt about Edwards's attacking Hanan? Explain your answer.

3. What does the final sentence of the story mean? What do you think life will be like for Louis and Margaret after Louis gets out of jail? *Can't survive*

Vocabulary

Choose the correct word. Write the completed sentences in your notebook.

1. Louis Edwards could not find work as a ___*B*___.
   a. doctor   b. head waiter   c. civil engineer

2. Edwards knew that a woman who is willing to face ___*A*___ for her husband's ideals is a treasure.
   a. poverty   b. strike   c. money

3. Cold gray eyes stared at him with something like ___*C*___.
   a. strike   b. contempt   c. poverty

4. The waiters who were on ___*A*___ were not at all happy about being replaced.
   a. strike   b. poverty   c. contempt

5. The men in the streets angrily shouted, "Yah! Yah! Old Adams hires ___*B*___!"
   a. women   b. Negroes   c. whites

Word Study

Write the sentences below in your notebook. Complete each sentence with the correct form of the word. Use the chart to help you. The first one has been done for you.

Verb	Noun	Adjective
clothe	clothing	clothed
amuse	amusement	amused
explode	explosion	explosive

1. Most people were wearing light _____clothing_____ because of the heat.
   clothing/clothed

2. Some of the children running on the street were poorly _____.
   clothe/clothed

3. Edwards's reply seemed to _____ the restaurant owner greatly.
   amuse /amusing

4. Edwards wanted to tell the man, "I am not here for your _____."
   amuse/amusement

5. Edwards did not have an _____ personality.
   explosion/explosive

6. The heat and the sense of failure entered his brain in a blinding _____.
   explode/explosion

Extension Activity

Civil Engineers

As you read, Louis Edwards had a dream. He wanted to work as a civil engineer. He had gone to school to study and prepare for this kind of work. Tragically, because he was African American, he was not able to get work.

A. Read about the work of a civil engineer.

> A civil engineer can have many different kinds of jobs. He or she can be involved with the planning, designing, and construction of bridges, roads, buildings, and other public places. Most civil engineers work for the government or for private companies. Today, people study civil engineering in college and get advanced degrees after college.

B. Make a list of jobs that you are interested in learning more about. Then choose one job. Use library books and the Internet to research information about the job. Work with a small group. Discuss the job with group members, and answer the following questions:

1. What is the title of the job you are interested in?

2. How much schooling do you need to get such a job?

3. Where are the places you could work?

4. What are the usual hours of work?

5. What might you find interesting about this kind of work?

Writing Practice

Write Interview Questions

In the story "Hope Deferred," Louis Edwards goes for a job interview. A good interviewer asks important **interview questions.** A good interviewer asks the kinds of questions that will get the information he or she needs.

Here are some questions the interviewer may have asked Louis Edwards.

- How did you learn about this job?

- Where did you go to school?

- What did you study?

Imagine that you own a bookstore. You want to hire a high school student to work in your bookstore on weekends. Think about what you might need to know about the student. Write a list of ten questions that you would use to interview the student. You might begin your list with the following questions:

- How did you learn about this job?

- Are you presently in school?

- Do you have any experience in this field?

Glossary

adjective: word that describes someone or something: *He likes <u>bright</u> colors. She is a <u>cheerful</u> person.*

adverb: word that tells you how, when, or where something happens. *The mail came <u>late</u> today.*

author: person who writes a story; writer

author's purpose: author's reason for writing something, such as to entertain or to inform

characterization: how an author creates characters, including describing what characters look like and relating their thoughts, feelings, and actions

characters: people or animals in a story

chronological order: the telling of events in a story in the order that they happened

comparison: words that tell how two things are alike or different

conflict: character's problem or struggle. Conflicts may take place between two characters, between a character and nature, or inside a character.

critic: person who gives his or her opinion of something; reviewer

description: words that describe someone or something, or tell what someone or something is like

foreshadowing: an author's hints or clues about what will happen in a story

horror story: story written to frighten the reader. Poe's "The Cask of Amontillado" is a horror story.

infer: make reasonable guesses about the meaning of something based on clues or facts; make inferences

interview: a talk in which one person asks questions and writes down the other person's answers

main character(s): the most important character or characters in a story. Main characters often change or learn something by the end of a story.

make inferences: make reasonable guesses about the meaning of something based on clues or facts; infer

metaphor: comparison of two things that are not like each other. *Love is a bird in flight.* 惯(暗)喻

115

monitor comprehension: 测试my,解程度 check your understanding as you read

noun: word that names something or someone. *The dog has soft fur. The soldier wore a uniform.*

novel: long work of fiction that has characters, plot, setting, and often a theme

opinion: a person's thoughts or feelings about a subject. An opinion is not a fact; it cannot be proved. Opinions *can* be supported by facts and reasons.

personification: giving human traits to an animal or an object. *The pine tree was asleep in the moonlight.*

plot: events of a story; what happens to the characters in a story

predict: make a reasonable guess about what will happen

review: an opinion of something, such as a book or play. Critics write reviews to rate the quality of something.

reviewer: person who writes an opinion about something; critic

setting: when and where the story happens; time and place of the story's action

short story: short work of fiction with characters, plot, setting, and sometimes a theme

simile: comparison between two things using the word *like*. Most similes compare unlike things. *His mind is like a sponge.*

skimming: reading very quickly to get a general idea of a text

summary: short review of the key information; brief retelling of a story's most important events and ideas

theme: central idea that an author expresses by telling a story. You can often state a theme in a sentence: *It's not easy to choose between two things you love.*

verb: word that describes an action *(We ate rice)* or a state *(We were sleepy)*

visualize: imagine, or picture, something in your mind
想像 视觉化

Index